VISITS TO SAINTS OF ❊ INDIA ❊

VISITS TO
SAINTS OF
✸ INDIA ✸

Sacred Experiences and Insights

Swami Kriyananda

Ⓠ crystal clarity **publishers**
Nevada City, CA 95959

Crystal Clarity Publishers, Nevada City, CA 95959

© 1973, 2019 by Hansa Trust
First Printing, 1973
Second Printing, 1975
Third Printing, 2018
All rights reserved.

"Anandamayee Ma" in Part I was originally published in
Ananda Varta, 1983. Part II was originally published in 1973 as
Letters from India, and reprinted in 1975 as
A Visit to Saints of India, by Ananda Publications, Nevada City, CA.

Printed in the United States

1 3 5 7 9 10 8 6 4 2

ISBN-13: 978-1-56589-321-4
eISBN-13: 978-1-56589-576-8

Cover designed by David Jensen and Amala Cathleen Elliott
Interior designed by David Jensen

[Library of Congress Cataloging-in-Publication data available]

Crystal Clarity Publishers
www.crystalclarity.com
clarity@crystalclarity.com
800.424.1055

❋ Contents ❋

❋ Publisher's Note ❋

SEVERAL OF THE SAINTS featured or mentioned in these pages were first introduced to Westerners through Paramhansa Yogananda's classic *Autobiography of a Yogi*.

The author of this book, Swami Kriyananda, was a close and direct disciple of Yogananda. During the time when Kriyananda wrote the letters published in Part I of this book, he was a minister and lecturer serving Yogananda's organization, Self-Realization Fellowship ("SRF"), which functions in India under the name of Yogoda Satsanga Society ("YSS"). At the time Kriyananda wrote the letters in Part II, he was no longer affiliated with SRF/YSS.

Sme of the other individuals mentioned in these letters—such as Rajarshi Janakananda, Daya Mata, Ananda Mata, etc.—were notable members of SRF, and, during the time these letters were written, Daya Mata was serving as its president.

References to "Master" are referring to Paramhansa Yogananda.

—Crystal Clarity Publishers

❋ Prologue ❋

INDIA! LAND OF GREAT saints and yogis. One has only to set foot on that sacred ground, if he is sensitive, to feel the blessings rising up therefrom. Fittingly did Paramhansa Yogananda end his life with the last words of his poem, "My India":

"I am hallowed; my body touched that sod!"

India is going through a period of transition, necessary for it as one of the great cultures of this world. She needs, for now, to reclaim her rightful place as a leader among nations. When I first went there, in 1958, there were still true saints to be found. I lived there, in all, nearly four years, with a six months hiatus in America and Europe in 1960. I returned, briefly, in 1972. Since then I came back several times as a visitor. Then in 2003 I came once more, to live and complete my Guru's work in this country. Over the course of these nearly fifty years, I have seen many changes. Not all of them are pleasing for one whose life is dedicated to seeking God. But I see that they are necessary. And I believe the sacred vibrations of India will rise triumphant, at last, over the mists of materialism that now swirl like brume upon the earth here.

During my first visit I had the privilege to meet many saints and holy people. On my later visit in 1972 I met fewer. During the past four years I have met fewer yet. I am doing what I can to bring India material prosperity as well as spiritual affluence. As I introduce my Guru's concept of "World Brotherhood Colonies," which by now I have well established in the West, I hope in time to cover the country with little communities where devotees live, work for God, raise families if that is their desire, and educate their children—all in a Godly way. The system has been proved by forty years of success. There are now about 1,000 people living in thriving Ananda Communities in America and in Italy.

9

May the following pages help to inspire people with a return to the spiritual living of India's ancient, Vedic times! For this is, indeed, the spirit of our Ananda communities in the West, and recognized as such by saints as well as by ordinary visitors to them from India. During my visits to saints during my first period in India, I wrote many letters about them to my brother and sister disciples in America. Most of those letters have been lost, or are now inaccessible. Those visits included several saints. One was an old yogi, 132 years in age, whom I met in Puri. I met several saints at the Kumbha Mela in Allahabad in 1960, among whom were Deohara Baba (aged 144 years, who told me he had known Lahiri Mahasaya); Kara Patri (mentioned in *Autobiography of a Yogi*); Hansa Maharaj, 122 years of age, who announced that he would leave his body in April of that year (in fact, he did so); and several other saints whose names I have forgotten.

I met, in New Delhi, a young woman who at the age of nine had announced to her parents that she was going into seclusion, and for them please not to disturb her, but to leave meals for her outside her door. From then on, she had eaten little, but had spent her time in prayer and meditation. Her only communication was by letter. When her family left notes outside her door requesting prayers for people, she would pray, and at least in most cases those prayers were granted.

Her father was chronically ill. Requests that she pray for his healing, however, were not accepted. She answered by note, "Prayers will not help him." At last her mother complained to her that she was showing a sort of reverse prejudice in not healing him, "Just because he is your father." The girl, then, had to agree to pray, but she said, "You will see what the outcome will be." She healed her father, but soon after that he began living a dissolute life. His illness had prevented that karma from coming out. She had wanted him to expiate the karma fully, but now he would have to go through it, and, later on, pay the full consequences.

I met her when she was nineteen. She still had the body of a young girl. She almost never came out of her room, but she came out for me, and meditated with me for a time.

Very soon afterward, she was seen weeping before her image of Krishna. The next day, she was dead.

I met also Bhupendranath Sanyal, or Sanyal Mahasaya, the oldest living disciple of Lahiri Mahasaya. This was at his ashram outside of Puri. It was a hallowed meeting, filled with mutual divine love.

I spent time at Gowardhan Math in Puri with Bharati Krishna Tirth, the Shankaracharya of that same Math. I had prepared his lecture tour in America in 1957 or '58.

I spent much more time with Anandamayee Ma than is indicated in the relatively brief episodes related in these pages. I used to call myself, and was known to many of her disciples, as her *"chhoto chele"* (little child). Truly, she was like a spiritual mother to me. I could have the sense of familiarity with her that I never had with my own Guru, whom I held too much in awe. Part of my difficulty was that I was so young. And part of it was simply that he was, truly, so commanding in his personality. (Ah, how I wish I could devote many pages to my precious visits with her!)

I found India less blessed with saints during my 1972 visit. And for these last four years, I have met very few. Those blessed days will come again, however. I am sure of it.

And I pray that my labors in this country will help significantly to speed their coming.

In divine friendship,

Swami Kriyananda
Guragon, India
October 13, 2007

Part I
Early Visits

❋ My First Meetings ❋ with Anandamayee Ma

February 1959

Originally published in Ananda Varta, *October 1983*

The following is based on a long letter I wrote—but never completed—to the SRF monks in Los Angeles, on notes that I made after each meeting with the Mother, and on accounts contributed by Mohini Chakravarty, an SRF/YSS devotee.

S RI DAYA MATA AND her party, consisting of Ananda Mata, Sister Revati, and myself, had been visiting Sri Yukteswar's seaside hermitage in Puri. On about February 9, we returned to the YSS Baranagar ashram outside Calcutta, where we were living. Soon after our arrival we learned that, during our absence, Anandamayee Ma had come to Calcutta.

What a thrill! Paramhansa Yogananda's beautiful account of her in *Autobiography of a Yogi* had inspired all of us, his disciples, with her example of divine love, with her ecstatic absorption in God's infinite bliss. One of our greatest hopes in coming to India had been that we would have the opportunity of meeting her. Now Divine Mother had brought her figuratively to our doorstep! We looked forward with keen anticipation to meeting her.

My own eagerness, however, was not unmixed with a certain anxiety. On Friday of that week I was scheduled to fly to Madras to lecture at the SRF/YSS center there. Would I be able to see the

Mother before then? It all depended on whether I could find someone to take me to her, as I had no way of getting there on my own.

On Wednesday evening, February 11, the four of us were sitting with two or three Indian friends around the dining room table. Talk turned (inevitably!) to Anandamayee Ma, and to our prospects for visiting her. "But," we lamented, "we've no idea where she's staying!"

"It must be in Agarpara," said Mohini Chakravarty, one of the friends who were present. "That's where she stays when she comes to Calcutta."

"Do you know how to get there?" I asked.

"Yes, I could take you."

"At what time does she generally see people?"

"At about this time."

This was not an opportunity to let slip away! I said, "Why don't we go there right away?"

My proposal was a bit sudden for the others in our party, but Mohini agreed to accompany me, and minutes later we were on our way.

I meditated as we drove through the darkness. A peculiar joy filled me. Did the Blissful Mother already know we were coming? Was she blessing me before I even met her?

"Mohini," I said, "please don't tell the Mother who I am (that is to say, a disciple of Paramhansa Yogananda, who was of course well known to the Mother's devotees). I don't want the formality of an introduction. Let me just slip quietly into the back of the room and sit there in meditation. That will be a sufficient joy for me." I wanted a spiritual, not a social, contact with the Mother. Also, I felt timid at the thought of representing Master before such an exalted being, unworthy disciple as I am. Better just to come in and sit unnoticed.

I saw her first through a series of French doors which ran the length of one wall of the assembly hall. At once, and every time I saw her again during the days to come—even in semidarkness, when I couldn't distinguish her features—I understood anew the meaning of Master's words when he wrote of the blessing that flows from the mere sight of a saint. There was no mistaking it. I was beholding a truly divine being.

I slipped quietly into the room and sat cross-legged on the floor at the back. There must have been about 150 people present. The Mother was speaking and laughing amiably. Her voice, as pure and bell-like as a little girl's, thrilled my heart. I closed my eyes in meditation. Soon I began to lose myself in inner peace and devotion.

After a time, the congregation stood up. The meeting had obviously come to an end. I couldn't bring myself to move or to open my eyes, but the people around me began talking, so I assumed that the Mother had left the room.

I hadn't wanted to be introduced to her, but now that she had retired I thought a little sadly, "It would have been nice to exchange just a glance with her—even a loving smile!" But she was gone now. And who was I, anyway, to expect any favors? I contented myself with the inner blessing I knew I'd received.

I continued meditating for several minutes. Then Mohini tapped me on the arm.

"I am going to inquire if the Mother can be persuaded graciously to come out again and meet you."

"No!" I exclaimed, "please don't! It would be too much of an imposition. Her evening with the public is over. Who am I to deserve special favors?"

But Mohini lovingly disregarded my reluctance. (He knew what I really wanted!) Approaching one of the Mother's devotees, he made his request. Presently word came back that she would see me. I went and stood by the door of her room, my heart beating with a mixture of dread and joy.

As I stood there, Sri Anil Ganguli, a devotee of the Mother, sounded a note of mock warning: "Beware of the cobra's poison. Once you get it into your system, you may never be able to get it out again!" Presently she came out. Sweetly she asked where I had come from, how long I had been in India, and a few questions of a general nature. I told her that I am a disciple of Paramhansa Yogananda, adding that, thanks to him, all of us in his ashrams in America felt great love for her.

At this she smiled appreciatively, then added quietly, "There is no love except the love of God. Without His love, it is not possible to love people."

This answer, and the way she uttered it, so thrilled me that I could make no reply, but only smiled happily.

After a few moments, she asked me when I was planning to return to America. I replied, "We'll all be going back to our ashram in April."

"'Our ashram'? Can you tell me where your ashram is, that you must go back to it?"

With a smile of appreciation, I corrected myself. "This body is my ashram, because it is here I sit for meditation."

"No. Why your body? Your body is temporary. Ashram is everywhere. It cannot be limited.

"In a spiritual sense," she continued, "the meaning of the word 'ashram' is, 'ar shram noy'—cessation from all compulsory activity. In this effortless divine state, all is perceived as one.

"In another sense, 'ashram' refers to the four stages of life [*brahmacharya, grihastha, vanaprastha,* and *sannyasa*]. But the Divine can be known in all of these states. So these, too, are all one. Everything is one—all one." (That last word, "one," she uttered in English, laughing merrily at her own use of a foreign word.)

Mohini said, "Brother Kriyananda asked me on our way here to let him just come in quietly and meditate, and not to tell you who he is."

The Mother, gazing at me quietly and affectionately, replied, "But I saw him come in, even though he was unannounced. I was watching him meditate.

"What do you mean, however, by the expression, 'Who he is'? Who is he, indeed, anyway? Who is anybody? This little girl (the Mother, I learned, generally referred to herself in this way) forgets herself so much she can't even remember who she is supposed to be! Occasionally, someone who has been close to this body for years will be sitting nearby, and I will ask, 'Where is So-and-so?', calling this person by name. Sometimes people are disappointed when I don't recognize them, but it is because I don't use this mind as others do. I am led by *kheyal*—by 'moods'!" (Again she used the English word, "moods," and laughed happily. By "moods," however, she didn't mean that she is moody in the ordinary, human sense. But just as human moods are irrational and unpredictable, so the kheyal is above reason and is not dependent upon the logical process for its perceptions and decisions. Kheyal may sometimes seem whimsical to the limited intellect, but it never is.)

The Mother mentioned that the following day was the festival of Saraswati *puja* (worship). Saraswati is the Hindu goddess of learning and music. The Mother urged me, if I could, to attend the function.

Mohini then told her that I could sing a few devotional songs in Bengali. She replied, "That is very nice. But it may not be possible to listen to them tomorrow. We shall certainly be able to hear them the following day."

"But," remonstrated Mohini, "our brother's difficulty is that he is scheduled to leave for Madras on Friday morning."

Impulsively I intruded: "I am supposed to leave then. But I am seriously considering postponing the journey."

Everyone, including the Mother, laughed appreciatively. Sri Ganguli remarked, "Aha! What did I say! The cobra poison has begun to take effect!" Everyone laughed again.

Mohini then relayed the wish of Daya Mata to meet the Mother privately. Because the Mother had not yet met Daya Ma, she somehow got the impression that it was I who wanted the appointment. "Father," she replied, "you know I do not like to bind myself with appointments. Once I make a promise, I must keep it regardless of all other considerations. Please speak to Swami Paramananda downstairs and ask him to make the appointment for me."

She rose to leave. With a full heart I thanked her in Bengali for having come out again especially to see me.

The Mother smiled. "'Thank you' is too formal," she remarked. (In Bengali the expression is used less frequently than in English, and has a formal ring to it: "dhanyawad.") "Will you thank your own self?" When I looked puzzled as to what I might offer as an alternative, she addressed Mohini: "Ask him, would he thank his own mother?"

"Yes," I replied after Mohini's translation, "in English it is customary to show appreciation in this way, even to our loved ones."

The Mother, smiling, then conceded, "Well, if it is customary with you, it is all right."

Lovingly she gave me a flower and a tangerine, upon which I said with a smile, "Now what can I say to you? Must I accept these in silence?"

She replied with a gentle laugh, "Say what you want. It is all the same."

I thanked her in English. (I guess I'm just too much of a Westerner!) Then, with a full heart, I said how happy I was to have met her. As she turned to go, I touched her feet lovingly. (Later I was to learn that it is strictly against the ashram rules for anyone to touch her feet. But no one, least of all the Mother herself, corrected me for my unwitting breach of etiquette.)

My heart was full. Eagerly I looked forward to the following day, when I planned to urge the rest of our group to come too, and attend Saraswati puja at the ashram.

Thursday, February 12, 1959

Daya Ma and the others had been planning to visit the Mother on Friday, but changed their minds on learning that Saraswati puja was a special day at the Agarpara ashram.

We arrived there at about eleven in the morning. Daya Ma was as anxious as I'd been to internalize the experience. She didn't want it turned into a ceremonial encounter between two heads of religious organizations. At her request, therefore, care was taken not to disclose her identity and those of the other sisters. The three of them took their seats a bit away from the crowd, and at a distance from the Mother. I sat at the back of the crowd.

Standing up at one point to locate the sisters, I caught the Mother's eye. Sitting down again, I found my meditation instantly deepening.

Public curiosity about us couldn't be stifled. When the puja ceremony had ended, people approached Prabhas-da (Master's cousin) and Mohini Chakravarty and asked who we were. Thus the truth came out. Daya Ma and the rest of us were immediately invited to come up on the platform and sit near the Mother, who blessed each of us, giving Mataji a garland and the rest of us roses.

Many people came forward for her blessings. One woman pressed many gifts on her, but not in a spirit of devotion. The Mother turned away from her to face us. Her magnetism drew us into a meditative state.

Then she asked me to sing. Nervously at first, I complied by singing Ram Proshad's beautiful song, in Bengali, "Will that day come to me, Ma, when crying, Mother! my eyes will flow with tears?" I soon lost myself in the inspiration of the words.

"Most beautifully sung!" exclaimed the Mother at the song's end. Turning to the crowd, she remarked concerning us, "They are soft!"

Then, rising, she told us, "Please remain seated. I will be away only for a little while."

After she'd left I sang Master's chant, "In the Valley of Sorrow," in English. She returned after I'd finished and told me, "I was listening to you. Please sing it again."

I did so, then sang two other songs in Bengali: "Blue Lotus Feet," and "Take Me on Thy Lap, O Mother!"

"What sweetness you express through your singing!" she exclaimed.

I said, "It gives me much joy to be able to sing for you," to which she replied:

"Joy cannot be measured in terms of 'much' or 'little.' It is absolute."

A devotee then sang a devotional song in Hindi. While the woman was singing, the Mother looked at Daya Ma long and deeply. Afterward, she remarked to the crowd, "Look, here you see an example of the unimportance of understanding the words literally. These Americans have not literally followed a single word of the Hindi song. But see how, overcome by the spirit of the song, water is flowing down their cheeks!" She tossed Daya Ma a garland, then gave us all garlands. Of Daya Ma she said, "She has come a long way to make this contact. Her meditative state is beautiful."

The time came at last for us to leave. Using the Bengali expression for "goodbye," I said, "*Tabe asi*" (literally, "Then I come again").

"To say you will come again," she replied with a gentle smile, "implies that we shall be separated for a while. But there can be no separation between us."

Friday evening, February 13

I postponed my trip to Madras, so as to take the fullest possible advantage of Mother's stay near Calcutta.

Friday evening I went again, accompanied by Mohini, but without the others. The Mother asked me to chant again. I sang "Blue Lotus Feet" and "Will That Day Come to Me, Ma?" Later, still under the impression that I, rather than Daya Ma, had requested an interview, she asked me if I didn't want to see her privately. At first, embarrassed to take up her time, I declined, but almost immediately corrected myself and said "Yes."

Mohini came into her interview room with me to act as a translator. But once we got there, I could think of nothing to say! Then I remembered that Brother Turiyananda, in America, had told me the only thing he wanted from India was Anandamayee Ma's blessings and some item that she had used. I made this request for him.

"Very well," she replied.

"Also," I continued, recalling a problem that was bothering me, "my sadhana has been a little difficult in recent weeks. Might I have your blessings and any advice that you'd care to give me?"

Mother: "Always think the divine grace is with you. Depend on it, and you will never find it wanting." She paused, then continued, "Now then, tell me what you want me to give you of my belongings."

I: "Mother, that is for you to say."

Mother: "No. Take anything—bed sheet, shawl—anything."

I hesitated.

She: "Will you be shy about asking from your own mother?"

I: "But please, I don't know what you need most."

She: "I don't need anything!"

I: "Please, at least let one of your devotees choose for you."

She: (firmly) "No, you must choose. Are you not my own?"

I: (wanting to make the smallest request possible) "Then Mother, might I have a handkerchief?"

An attendant rose instantly to fetch one for me. Thinking suddenly how nice it would be to have a memento of my own, I said hastily, "Mother, might I have *two* handkerchiefs?" Everyone laughed.

Mother: (taking off her shawl and giving it to me) "Here, this is for you. I have worn it for five years." She gazed at me lovingly. Then, in her "mood" to give me more, she ordered the attendant to bring me a flower bouquet also. Of the shawl, she told me, "Wrap your body with this shawl, but always remember that *Nama*— God's Name—is the best thing in which to wrap yourself."

Overcome with emotion, I held the shawl silently to my heart for some moments. Then I told her, "We all feel we are not meeting you for the first time."

Mother: "The more you advance in meditation, the more you will realize your identity with me."

I: "Mother, would you give me some personal advice for my spiritual practice?"

She: "Always practice *japa*. Keep your mind busy chanting God's name, and you won't have time to think of anything else. Say, 'Hari! Hari!'"—here she clapped her hands joyfully once, as if to indicate that everything of this world disappears with the thought of God—"or any other mantra you like. Filled with His joy, you will laugh at all dangers."

I: "I like to take my Guru's name."

She: "That is good. Everything you have attained has come to you through his blessings."

I was so full of inner joy by this time that I could only close my eyes in meditation. While I meditated, the Mother spoke briefly with Mohini. He told her that I and the others in our party meditated five or six hours a day.

Mother: "I can see that. Your American brother and sisters are highly advanced in the spiritual path. Daya Ma, especially, enjoys perfect calm, both inside and outside."

I: "Mother, you are so good!"

Mother: (sweetly) "It takes goodness to see goodness."

She gave me the bouquet she had ordered and the handkerchief, adding to them a large towel. Love filled my heart.

"*Tomar chele khub kusi*," I said as we left, meaning, "Your child is very happy!"

Saturday, February 14

We went again to Agarpara this evening. Mother asked me to sing "Blue Lotus Feet" for her again. I sang it gladly.

Mother: "How many times I have asked him to sing this song! In spite of so many repetitions, it never loses its charm."

Later I told her, "Daya Ma would like to spend some time with you alone—not to talk; just to meditate."

Mother: "She is always welcome."

I had brought a scarf to give her. Hesitantly I gave it at last, whereupon she said playfully, "I was going to snatch it from you, but waited to see if you would give it!" She then asked me to put it around her shoulders.

When I had done so, she repeated ten times, solemnly, "*Tomar ghare ami thaki*"—"I dwell in your heart (literally, 'room')."

"I know," I said, thinking of a blessing I had received from her in meditation that morning. I added, "*Ami tomar chele*—I am your child."

She: "This is not a new relationship. It is eternal."

I: "I know." I was thinking both in the human sense, and of her as a manifestation of the Divine Mother.

ტ჻ ტ჻ ტ჻ ტ჻ ტ჻ ტ჻ ტ჻ ტ჻

In time I became known affectionately as her "*chhoto chele*— little child."

Many were the meetings we had over the months and years after that. Always she showered me with grace. One time she said, "Many thousands have come to this body. None have attracted me as you have." The translators emphasized several times to me that she had said, "None."

Another time she said, "There are people who have been with me for twenty-five years and more, but they haven't taken from me what you have."

And to others I'm told she once said, "Here is a lotus in a pond. Many frogs sit under the lotus, croaking. Then a bee flies in, takes the honey, and flies away. Kriyananda is that bee."

She surprised me once by asking, "What would you say if I asked you to stay here?" Why did she ask me that? Perhaps she saw what I would suffer from my Guru's organization. But even had I known what the future would bring, I would have faced that suffering rather than forsake my dedication to him. Perhaps she didn't want me to devote my life to service, but purely to sadhana. I could have remained faithful to Master in her ashram. Certainly she would not have asked me to leave him; that is not her way. But I couldn't set aside his words to me: "Your life is one of intense activity—and meditation"; his statement, "Your work is lecturing and writing"; and his frequent charge to me, "You have a great work to do." Moreover, I had dedicated this incarnation to spreading his work. I live for nothing else.

After my separation from SRF, Anandamayee Ma later told me, she would gladly have taken me in. But Master himself seems to have prevented that possibility, for I was not granted an Indian visa for ten years.

Nevertheless, Anandamayee Ma occupies a more than special place in my heart. I see her as the Divine Mother Herself. Through her, next to Master, I have received the greatest blessings in my life. Indeed, with her I was able to have the relationship that my greenness on the path never permitted me to have with Master during his lifetime. It was a relationship which, far from taking me from my Guru, served to deepen my relationship also with him.

Swami Kriyananda meditating with Anandamayee Ma

Yogi Ramiah (Sri Rama Yogi) and the author

❊ A Visit to Yogi Ramiah ❊

Forethoughts

I WAS WITH MY GURU at his Twenty-Nine Palms retreat in the spring of 1950. One day he addressed me in words that have appeared lately in my book, *Conversations with Yogananda*, from Saying #87:

"Very few saints," he said, "have attained final liberation."

I exclaimed in dismay, "What about all those saints in the *Autobiography*? Are all of them dead, with no one else to replace them?" (In *Autobiography of a Yogi*, Paramhansa Yogananda makes it clear that final liberation is usually attained from higher astral worlds, and not from this material plane. It seemed to me, however, on hearing his statement, that this highest goal must be virtually impossible of attainment. And yet, interestingly—as I have quoted him in another of my books, *The Path**—he told us in either 1948 or 1949, during the Christmas meditation at Mt. Washington, "Of those present, there will be a few *siddhas* [fully liberated souls], and quite a few *jivan muktas* [free in God, though with some past karma still to work out].")

"Very few even of those saints" (those in the *Autobiography*), he replied, "were fully liberated."

I named several of them specifically. In response to each name he answered, "Not yet." Finally he said, "The only ones fully liberated were Babaji, Lahiri Mahasaya, Sri Yukteswarji, and two of Lahiri

---

* He later revised the book, and retitled it *The New Path.*—Publisher's note

Mahasaya's disciples: Swami Pranabananda [the 'Saint with Two Bodies'] and Ram Gopal Muzumdar [the 'Sleepless Saint']."

"What about your father?"

"Oh, he was too much attached to us, as his sons."

"What about Mataji, the sister of Babaji? I recall you stated in the *Autobiography* that she was 'almost as great' as Babaji."

"Well, that means she was not yet fully liberated. Still, she must be so by now. Otherwise, only those I have mentioned."

"What about Trailanga Swami?"

"No, not even he."

(On the occasion quoted here, Master didn't name himself. At other times, however, he told us that he had come into this body fully liberated—many lifetimes ago.)

"I also met another fully liberated soul," Master added. "His name was Yogi Ramiah. He was a disciple of the great master, Ramana Maharshi. It does occasionally happen that a disciple becomes more highly advanced than his guru."

Master described how, when he had met Yogi Ramiah, the two of them had walked about the grounds, hand in hand, steeped in God's love. "Oh," Master exclaimed, "if I had stayed half an hour longer in his company, I could not have brought myself to leave India again. *He* was the real India that I love.

"Years later, he materialized before Paul Brunton and asked him for my photograph."

I asked Master, "Why can't an enlightened master simply dissolve all his karma the moment he realizes his oneness with God?"

"Well," Master replied, "in that state you don't really care. You see all this as a dream. You may even go on for incarnations that way, descending to earth in order to bring your disciples freedom. At that level of development, masters may even deliberately keep a little bit of karma to hold them down to this play for a while for that higher purpose. Once you've attained the highest state of *nirbikalpa samadhi,* no ego-consciousness remains. Your soul is essentially free, anyway."

"What is it, Master," I asked, "that draws a soul back to earth after one has attained final liberation?"

My Guru replied, "Some siddhas still keep the 'desireless desire' to help others." (A "desireless desire" is one that is self-expansive, and not focused on the little ego. It is directed toward helping others. Thus, it creates no ego-bondage. A desireless desire must not be understood, therefore, as one that is merely trivial. My Guru once said to me, "Every desire must be fulfilled." I asked in some consternation, "*Every* desire, Master? Even a fleeting wish for an ice cream cone?" "Oh yes!" he replied with emphasis.)

I asked Master, perhaps on the same occasion, why he hadn't included his visit to Ramana Maharshi and Yogi Ramiah in his autobiography. He answered, "Because Paul Brunton already wrote beautifully about his own visit in *A Search in Secret India.*"

The following letter about Yogi Ramiah (Sri Rama Yogi) was one I wrote to Sri Daya Mata after my four-day visit to him at his ashram near Nellore.

November 10, 1960

Dear Daya Mata:

Your Pinocchio* is back in Madras after several days in Nellore. Now I am going to Kodaicanal for a few days of seclusion.†

---

* I used this name in the recollection of how my father had applied it to me, after a long letter I'd written about a trip I had taken to Mexico in 1945, when I was nineteen. My parents were in Romania at the time. My father had been posted there after World War II, as the petroleum attaché for the U.S. diplomatic mission to that country.

† This, too, was something of a miracle. I found myself stuck in that Madras hotel, unable to get out of town owing to the floods, but wanting a place to go for seclusion. Finally, one morning, I prayed in desperation to Babaji for help. After meditating I went down to the dining room for breakfast. A new couple I hadn't met before were sitting at the table next to mine. The husband announced to me, as if out of the blue, "I'd like to invite you to spend some time in seclusion at our house in Kodaicanal. The house is empty, and will remain so for two or three more weeks until our return. You'd be very welcome to stay there."

My visit to the Nellore area was simply wonderful. I was a guest of Yogi Ramiah (Sri Rama Yogi, as he is known now) at his ashram in the nearby village of Annareddipalayam, somewhat beyond a slightly larger and better-known village, Bucchireddipalayam. I found him an immense inspiration.

I have been confined in Madras for most of my time in the south of India, by record rains and floods—the worst in thirty or forty years, so the newspapers tell us—that have prevented many trains and buses from leaving the city. At last I was informed that a train would be going to Nellore. I eagerly seized this opportunity.

It was quite a trip. First- and second-class coaches were all filled up. All I could get was a third-class ticket. Then I discovered that all the third-class coaches were full almost to overflowing. At last I found a seat in a little compartment reserved for the servants of first-class passengers. Asked if I was a servant, I replied, "Certainly. I am a servant of God!"

It was a tight squeeze, especially as more people in the same predicament as mine came pouring in like water though a gap in a dam. The tiny compartment had a sign posted, "To seat five persons." Seventeen of us were crammed in there! The trip turned out, moreover, to be circuitous, as the main line had been washed away by floods. Instead of taking the scheduled four hours, it took us nine and a half hours to reach Nellore. (How I pitied those poor people in this compartment who were going all the way to Delhi!) As for myself, though my body got bruised all over because of my cramped position on that hard wooden bench, I remained happily chanting the whole time in my heart to God and Guru.

In Nellore I spent the night in a cheap hotel. The next morning I took a taxi to Ramashram in the village of Annareddipalayam, where Yogi Ramiah lives. I had not been able to notify him of my coming in advance, since the floods had made planning completely uncertain.

And so I arrived, unheralded and (I imagine) unexpected. I found no one there who spoke English, so Yogi Ramiah sent me all the way back to Nellore (about thirteen miles) with a written note to a disciple of his, a Professor Padmanabha Rao, requesting him to come and translate for us. The professor is a young man, very good hearted, and blessed with considerable discrimination and a keen intelligence. He obligingly canceled his classes for the rest of that day, and applied for a leave of absence for the rest of the week. Thus, he was able to come out with me and translate my discussions with the saint. Imagine such kindness! Of course, Professor Rao was also glad for the excuse to be with his guru.

I found Sri Rama Yogi by nature extremely withdrawn, hiding his spiritual glory from a wish to avoid curiosity seeking. Professor Rao told me his guru sometimes will even scold people somewhat sharply, if they are merely superficial seekers, as a means of discouraging them from coming back.

He has a way, I found, of sitting and gazing off into the distance as though unaware of anyone around him. He himself told me that, when conversing with people, he usually confines himself to inconsequential talk about such matters as food, the weather, and conditions in the country. If one uses discrimination, however, he will see, lambent within the eyes of Sri Rama Yogi, a hidden divine laughter, and a flow of such deep, divine love that, for me at least, when the time came to leave him four days later, I felt like weeping.

I was housed in the ashram above the room where Swamiji (as he is also called) practiced sadhana for years. The grounds round about used to be the village cremation area. (In those years this area was quite secluded. Now, the village has encroached around the grounds, and has brought with it some of the noise and business of communal life.) Sri Rama Yogi built a small house there years ago, which he used for meditation. For years he spent most of his time doing spiritual practices, eating little (his daily diet being one apple, one orange, and one glass of milk). He lost a lot of weight during that time, but that meager diet helped his efforts at concentration.

One night a curious villager crept up to the little structure and peeked through a small chink in the wall. He beheld Yogi Ramiah seated inside, surrounded by a halo of blazing light. Amazed, the man remained there, staring. Gradually the light diminished, then vanished. Yogi Ramiah came out and addressed him: "You had better not gaze too long into this light. It may harm you." From this time on, the villagers have held Sri Rama Yogi in great awe.

After some years of practice, he achieved a state of meditative consciousness that he was not able to explain. His guru, who had taught him his practice, was no longer living. Rama Yogi knew of no one to resolve his dilemma. He first approached a number of pundits, asking them, "Is it possible that he who observes the Divine Light, his act of observing it, and the Light itself are actually one and the same thing?"

All of them replied, "Of course not! The very fact that something is seen indicates there must be a person viewing it. The person seeing, the act of seeing, and the object seen are obviously different. How, then, could they be identical?"

After some years, Sri Rama Yogi heard about the great sage Ramana Maharshi. Still seeking a solution to his problem, he went to Arunachala, where Ramana Maharshi lived. There, he entered and sat at the master's feet. Those present in the room felt greatly attracted to this young man of glowing countenance. They marveled, however, when he put his question to the master.

Ramana Maharshi smiled, then referred the question for comment to a scriptural scholar who was present. This man, a well-known pundit, replied as the others had done: "How can these things be identical? The one seeing, his act of seeing, and what he sees must obviously be separate. They cannot possibly be the same."

Ramana Maharshi then said, "No, Punditji, you are mistaken. There comes a state wherein all three of these—seer, seeing, and seen—are perceived as one reality."

Sri Rama Yogi thereupon accepted Ramana Maharshi as his guru. Remaining much of the time in the ashram, he observed *maun* [silence], and endeavored to remain always engrossed in that state of inner upliftment. It was some time after this, while he was still practicing *maun*, that our own Guru met him.

Nowadays, Sri Rama Yogi lives in virtual seclusion. I asked our Guru once whether the yogi had any disciples.

"He must have," Master said. "One cannot attain freedom until he has raised up at least six others."

Certain it is, however, that the Swamiji has very few disciples. Only one of them lives with him now: an old man, who is also his relative.

I asked Swamiji if he did not want to help others. "Who is to help whom?" he inquired. "God is the Doer. Even the urge to help is inspired by Him." I am not quoting him exactly here, and believe that he said more on the subject. Basically his answer was, "God has done what He wants to do with this body." Having merged his ego in the divine Self, Sri Rama Yogi acts now only as God directs him— or, putting it more in his own terminology, as he is inspired to do by the higher Self. His whole life declares that the purpose of life is one only: to remain immersed in the true Self within.

Meditation, Swamiji says, should be one's chief activity. What is the use, he asks, of going about doing religious propaganda, egoically inspired? The true spiritual search is internal. Even service to the guru, he proclaims, falls off when the seeker attains samadhi.

He told me that once, seeing others of the disciples serving Ramana Maharshi lovingly, he wondered if he couldn't serve in this way also. Ramana Maharshi discouraged him. "Those who need to serve the guru outwardly," he said, "belong to a lower order of disciple. Service helps to purify the heart and mind, and enables one to achieve internal communion. Once one has reached that plane, however, what point is there in performing actions of which the only spiritual purpose is to help the devotee to reach that state? You are rendering me the highest service by remaining immersed in samadhi. Seek only, therefore, to become completely identified with that Infinite Consciousness."

If people still have action karma to work out, then of course they must engage in appropriate outward activity. Service, in such cases, can be helpful. Gradual internalization, however, is the ultimate purpose of all such activity.

From a desire to understand Sri Rama Yogi's meaning more clearly, I mentioned the numbers of sadhus who think to achieve the divine goal by meditation alone, but who, being unable to meditate either long or properly, become lazy. In the end, I quoted my Guru as saying, they become good for nothing—or, to use his colorful expression, "they become bums."

"You are quite right!" Swamiji replied. "If I had such sadhus living in this ashram, I would put them to work in the garden. We must not lose sight, however, of the fact that meditation is the most important thing, and that the entire purpose of *any* sadhana—whether that of service, or of organizing, or of meditation—is to still the waves of the mind, and thereby to realize the Self within. The mind should always, therefore, be directed inwardly. If one is sincere, God will ultimately free him from every outward activity, enabling him to identify himself fully with the Self within."

At one point the Swamiji asked, "What about Daya Mata? What are her responsibilities?" (Evidently he has had some correspondence with you.) I explained what those duties are.

"Oof, what a burden!" he exclaimed as if commiseratingly.

"But surely, Swamiji," I replied, "that burden must have its compensations. Otherwise we would be forced to the conclusion—unacceptable, surely—that she was made the president only because of her bad karma!" I went on slightly teasingly, "We might even say that the main criterion for becoming president is that one's karma be sufficiently bad!"

He smiled as he replied, "Of course, it is her good karma! The intense activity she performs enables her to burn up her store of action karma more quickly, and helps her to gain release from it sooner than she would otherwise do. This doesn't mean, however, that others, in order to find God more quickly, too, might be equally helped by being given the same position! They themselves might find God sooner by performing little or no executive activity. In her case, your guru has given her this responsibility because this is the type of karma she has to work out. Thus, you see, it is her good karma to have this position, but it is so only because this is how she, specifically, needs to work out her own karmic patterns in the shortest time possible."

"Swamiji," I said, "you decry the necessity for religious propaganda. But you must mean only if it is inspired egoically. You cannot mean that one should not lecture if he has been instructed to do so by his guru. To my mind, the most important thing on the spiritual path is to please one's guru."

"Certainly you are right!" he replied. "Guru is everything. No matter what he tells you to do, you should do it with full willingness and enthusiasm."

He then went on to relate two stories concerning the merit of utter faithfulness to the guru's instructions. The first story was about a young man who approached a saint and asked to be received as his disciple. The master, after accepting him, sent him out into the pasture to tend the ashram cattle.

After six months, the guru came out into the field and asked his new disciple, "What are you doing for food?"

The young man replied, "Well, Master, every morning I go to the village and beg a little food from various households. With that small amount, I am getting along quite nicely."

The guru pursed his lips. "Consider those poor householders, however. Haven't they difficulty enough as it is, supporting their families and meeting endless expenses? Do you think it quite fair to add to their burden by begging food from them?"

The disciple took this gentle reprimand as a command to cease from asking others to feed him. From then on, he never again went out for his meals.

Six months later his guru again came to the pasture and asked what the disciple was doing for food.

"After milking the cows," the young man explained, "I go around to each of them and take what little milk is left in each udder. With that amount I am managing to get along very well, Master."

The guru frowned. "That little amount, however," he said, "may still be needed by the calves. Are they getting enough nourishment? And is it truly proper, do you feel, to take what belongs rightfully to them?"

All this while the guru offered no positive suggestions as to what his poor disciple might do to feed himself. The disciple, however, took this second reproach cheerfully, as his guru's wish. He therefore gave up taking any more milk from the cows' udders for himself.

Six months passed. Then the guru came out again and inquired of his disciple, "How are you getting your meals?"

"Guruji," the young man replied, "I am doing very well. While the calves suckle, a little foam gathers on the udders and drips down. I catch this foam in a cup, and with that I am getting all the nourishment I need."

"Ah, but I wonder. Whoever heard of foam gathering on an udder when the calf is suckling? These calves are surely doing this out of love for you, so that you too may be fed. In so doing, however, they are depriving themselves."

On hearing these words, the disciple stopped gathering even foam from the cows' udders.

Another six months passed. The guru again came out and asked, "What are you doing for food?" This time, the disciple said he was plucking fruit from the trees. The guru questioned the rightness even of this act. "Consider," he said. "You are depriving the birds of the forest."

Six months later the guru again came out to the pasture. This time, the disciple said he was eating the young shoots of grass and of other plants. The guru's pity for the young growing things, however, was hint enough to the disciple that he must desist even from this practice.

At last the young man took to eating leaves that had already fallen onto the ground from the bushes and trees. Unfortunately, he had the bad luck one day to eat a few leaves that had fallen from a poisonous plant. In consequence, he became blind. Because of his blindness, moreover, he lost his way and stumbled into a well.

In this predicament, too, all his thoughts concerned the safety of his guru's cattle. Would they arrive home all right without him?

Seeing the young man's steadfastness, the gods themselves assumed human form, and, gathering about the well, gazed down at him, marveling. The young man, hearing voices above him, didn't call out first to be lifted out of the water. Instead, he asked, "What has happened to my guru's cattle? Are they safely back in their shed?"

On hearing this question, the gods wondered at the disciple's unswerving obedience to his guru's wishes. Only now the guru hurried out, lifted his disciple from the well, and blessed him. Then it was, at last, that he bestowed on the faithful disciple the experience of the highest state of consciousness.

The other story Sri Rama Yogi told me was of a young disciple who was sent by his guru to gather wood for the kitchen from the village. The disciple performed this task day after day with one-pointed devotion, never considering how even the years were passing.

One day he dropped a fresh load of wood onto the ground in the ashram courtyard. A little tuft of hair on his head got caught between two logs, and was pulled out. Now, for the first time, he saw his hair, and realized that it had turned completely white.

He was aghast! Suddenly it dawned on him that many years had passed, and that he had become an old man. "And all this time," he reflected sorrowfully, "I have done nothing but haul wood for the ashram! I haven't learned any of the great truths for which I came seeking. I haven't attained any of those high states of consciousness for which I longed so deeply. All I have done has been to carry wood, which my guru asked me to bring from the village!"

Thinking these thoughts, he began to shed tears of sorrow.

At that very moment the guru rushed out of the house. Hastily he stretched out his hand to catch the first teardrop as it fell. "Don't you know," he cried, lovingly, "that if any tear of sorrow from such a great soul as you have become were to touch the ground, the people throughout this countryside would suffer famine for years to come? Dear one, don't weep. Do you not yet realize what you have attained by your years of single-minded service here?"

After uttering these words, the guru touched his disciple on the forehead. The "young man," now old, entered instantly into the highest samadhi, wherein he realized all knowledge, all wisdom, and eternal bliss as his very own.

"So you see," Sri Rama Yogi went on, "doing your guru's will is undoubtedly your highest sadhana. Even so, and above everything else, remember that his will for you is that you become immersed in the Self. All actions he has enjoined on you are only to help you to reach that state. The more you have of ecstasy, the less need you will have to be concerned with outer activities. Meanwhile, do your best to live always in the Self within."

(Indeed, Master once told me, "Always live in the Self. Come down a little bit to eat or speak, as necessary. Then withdraw again into the Self.")

I then commented to Swamiji, "My attitude in that matter is not one of wanting to be freed from activity that I might engage solely in meditation. My Guru came into the world in this life with a divine mission to fulfill. He needs my help, and that of many others, that his mission may be carried to completion. My feeling is that even if helping him means deferring my salvation to another life, in this lifetime I want to devote myself to doing all I can to help him with this sacred undertaking."

The Swamiji smiled. "And are you a separate agent from God, that you should think *you* must do something to help Him? Is this your work, or His?"

"May I not think," I replied, "that it is He who is inspiring me with this enthusiasm for His work?"

"Certainly. Enthusiasm is an excellent quality. Don't you see, however, that you will be able to do much more to further your guru's work as you deepen your divine attunement? Then, even with a minimum of effort, you will be able to do far more good than you can do now."

Here, of course, I had to agree. I recalled how Master had said of Rajarshi that, even in samadhi, he was doing untold good for the work through the blessings he attracted to it. And I recalled, further, how often my own enthusiastic activities, because they were not rooted in wisdom, resulted in nothing, but had only represented long days and nights of labor that might have been spent more constructively in deepening my sadhana. I remembered, moreover, how Master had been pleased with me when he felt that I was developing devotion, or other spiritual qualities. He had never shown as much pleasure in any work that I'd done as he had in the spirit with which I had done it.

Sri Rama Yogi said also, "Ask yourself always, 'Who am I?'" [This was a practice Ramana Maharshi particularly recommended.] I felt some hesitation on this point, and commented, "That wasn't the emphasis my Guru placed in his teachings to us."

Swamiji commented on both this statement and our preceding discussion: "It is not always easy for disciples to grasp the true import of their gurus' instructions. Were it so, there would not be all the confusion one encounters in religion today."

I remembered, then, that Master often told us we needed to distinguish between our little egos and the one true, divine Self.

"Whether you accept karma yoga as your means to inner purity," Sri Rama Yogi continued, "or practice long hours of meditation, you should strive to become ever more deeply immersed in the inner, divine consciousness. And when ecstasy comes, it will be infinitely preferable, even as a service to your guru, to the activities in which you are now engaged.

"Therefore I say to you, when ecstasy, or when deep meditative states come to you, do not tell yourself, 'I have work to do!' A lower duty must not take precedence over a higher duty. When deep meditation comes, forget everything else, at least for that time. It would even be preferable, if for example at such times you have a lecture to give, to cancel that lecture. You cannot give money away in charity if you haven't any to give. The more you have of God, the more you'll be able to inspire and uplift others. You will be sharing what you already have of Him. Moreover, unless your lectures inspire and uplift people, what good can they accomplish? The more you become filled with divine consciousness, the more you will find that, even uninvited by publicity, people will flock to hear you. I repeat, therefore: When meditation is deep, become lost in it. That is your highest duty."

Swamiji then gave me further words of advice.

"Do not practice more than one mantra, nor make more than one *chakra* the focal point of your concentration. If you divide the mind, you won't be able to bring it to a proper focus. Have only one mantra, one *ishta devata* [spiritual ideal], one focal point of concentration."

"Sir," I asked, "is it not good to concentrate on, and enjoy, the love that fills the heart during meditation?"

"If the heart is where you concentrate, it is all right. But if not, you will simply divide your concentration."

"But can I not then channel that feeling upward to the point between the eyebrows?"

"I still say," he replied, "it is better to be one pointed. And the best point on which to concentrate is the point between the eyebrows, although the heart also is good. Choose only one of them. Don't divide your attention. If you concentrate at the point between the eyebrows, *bhakti* [devotion] will be there, too. It is not as though devotion will be lacking. I repeat, then: Be one pointed.

"Another important point is to be regular in the times you set aside for meditation. Keep steadily to those same times every day.

"Another thing: Cut down on eating. Also, speak less. But this counsel is more general. I see that you are good in these respects, for you eat little, and you enjoy silence. These are great aids to *sadhana* [spiritual practice].

"The *shastras* [scriptures] teach that one should concentrate primarily, in one's choice of food, on the qualities one wants to gain from it. The chemical values of food are secondary in importance, particularly for *sadhakas* [spiritual seekers]. Every food has a particular effect on the mind. Thus, one's state of consciousness depends to a very marked degree on what one eats. If one consumes tamasic foods, he will tend to develop *tamas* [to become lazy, and heavy in consciousness]. If one eats *sattwic* foods, he will find it easier to develop spiritually. That is why fruits are enjoined, and cow's milk (as opposed to buffalo or goat), and why heavily spiced foods are best shunned."

At one point in our discussions I turned to a subject of less immediately practical import. It related to a question I'd entertained regarding something Master had once said to me: "When a soul becomes fully liberated, seven generations, forward and backward, in that person's family become liberated also." I'd been puzzled by the inequity of so many relatives getting liberated without any personal effort on their own part. Besides, I thought, what about his statement that a person can be liberated only after freeing at least six others? Did it seem quite fair of God, I thought, that He would "promote" anyone who had uplifted no one else, merely for getting born into the family of a great saint?

Sri Rama Yogi agreed with me. "Rather," he explained, "it is like when someone becomes an emperor or a president. That person's relatives often receive higher positions, both socially and economically, in consequence of his appointment. So it is that the relatives of a *param mukta* receive great stimulus in their own spiritual search, or become lifted to higher astral realms after they die, or receive good karma to varying degrees depending on their own receptivity. They do not, however, receive full liberation. For that supreme blessing, everyone must work! Without personal effort, no soul can ever escape *maya's* net.

"The blessings," he added, "go not only to the direct line of relatives, but also to cousins and to those in more distant branches. So even if one has no immediate progeny—and most saints are renunciates, and therefore beget no children—those seven generations may carry through other lines of descent in the family."

Swamiji went on to relate a charming story, one not directly connected to the preceding discussion. I'll tell it as clearly as I am able.

A famous saint named Namdev used to worship Lord Krishna's *murti* [image] outwardly in a temple. So deep was his devotion that Krishna actually spoke to him through that image. Many devotees, inspired by this saint, used to flock to him and sit at his feet for spiritual instruction.

Well, in the same town there lived another saint, a potter by profession, who used also to commune with Krishna through that temple *murti*. One day a large gathering convened in the temple to celebrate some important spiritual festival. This potter-saint, acting on a divine "whim," decided to test the spirituality of those who were assembled.

A potter's way of testing the soundness of a clay pot is to strike it with his knuckles. From the resulting sound, he can tell whether there is any crack in that pot. This potter-saint, accordingly, went among those assembled devotees and slapped each of them in turn. Because they all considered him a saint, they accepted this unusual behavior without remonstration, confident that there must be some deep purpose behind the act.

When the potter arrived at Namdev, he gave him a slap, too. Namdev wasn't this man's disciple, and was, besides, looked up to by everyone in that crowd as a saint. "How dare you do that?" he demanded of the potter indignantly.

Unperturbed, the potter stood up and announced, "There seems to be a crack in this pot." Everyone laughed, though perhaps with some embarrassment. Namdev himself was mortified.

Later on, he repaired to the sanctuary where the *murti* of Krishna was, and expressed his grievance. "Lord," he said, "You know that I love You. Why did You permit me to be so humiliated before all those devotees?"

Sri Krishna replied, "I'm sorry, Namdev, but the potter was right. There *is* a crack in that pot, somewhere."

"In that case, Lord, what can I do about it?"

"Namdev, you need the help of a guru."

"But I see You before me, You, the Lord of the universe! What need have I for a guru? Why don't You Yourself free me, Lord, of all imperfections?"

"My child," Krishna replied, "I can instruct and inspire you. To achieve freedom from all delusion, however, it is My law that you must receive the blessing of a true guru."

"Well, Lord, in that case, won't you please direct me to that guru who will help me out of the meshes of *maya?*"

The Lord directed Namdev to a certain village. "A great saint lives there," he said. "He is the guru for you. Don't be surprised, however," added the Lord, smiling, "if he seems a little strange. That is just his way."

Namdev made his way to that village, and inquired there concerning the whereabouts of the man Krishna had described to him.

"What, *that* lunatic?" people exclaimed. "What could you possibly want from *him?*" Finally, they dismissively indicated the general direction of the temple. "You'll probably find him sleeping up there. That's where he usually stays."

Namdev went to the temple. There he saw, lying on the floor, what appeared to be an old tramp, his hair disheveled, his clothing in disarray. To Namdev's particular horror, however, the old man had his feet resting on a *Shiva lingam*! Such an act of desecration was, for a *bhakta* like Namdev, simply unconscionable. Forgetting that this recumbent figure might be his guru, he strode over and loudly demanded that the man remove his feet from that holy image.

The old man glanced up sleepily and replied, "Young man, the difficulty is, I'm so old, I find it difficult to change my position. Please, would you move my feet to some place where there is no *lingam*?" Instantly Namdev raised the man's feet, and was about to place them down somewhere else when, to his astonishment, another *lingam* appeared in that spot also. Amazed, he once more lifted the man's feet and moved them, only to find another *lingam* where he'd been prepared to place them. As many times as he shifted the man's feet, another *lingam* appeared. (How, indeed, can the Lord's presence ever be confined in any one spot?)

Namdev understood at last. Humbly he prostrated himself before this old man, whom he now recognized to be his guru. "I understand, now," he said. "Will you accept me as your disciple?"

The guru stood up in full strength and dignity, and blessed Namdev with the Divine Vision. From then on, after leaving his guru Namdev roamed about the countryside, ever immersed in the omnipresence of God, whom he beheld everywhere and in everything. Thus, it never even occurred to him to return to the temple where he had worshiped before, and to offer there his thanks to Krishna. Day after day he roamed, drunk with the bliss of God. It was by chance only, one day, that he found himself back at the temple where Krishna had used to appear to him. He then went inside. And there Krishna appeared to him, as before.

"Where have you been, my child?" asked the Lord. "For six months you have not come to see me—you, who came to me every day. I have missed you!"

"O Lord!" cried Namdev. "How could I think of seeking You out here, when everywhere I looked, I could see nothing but You!"

Blissfully, then, the Lord smiled. "Now, Namdev, there are no more cracks in that pot!"

"So," Sri Rama Yogi went on to state, "if even as great a devotee as Namdev needed a guru to help him to attain the Supreme Vision, how could anyone attain that state without effort on his own, merely because some relative, possibly not even known to him, has attained it?"

My days with this great saint passed happily. I felt immense inspiration in his presence. Before returning to my work in Calcutta, however, I still felt a need for a few days of silence and solitude for meditation and introspection. Swamiji's ashram is surrounded by the noisy village. He himself has said he has been thinking of leaving it, and of going to spend his last days in the Himalayas. Throngs of people gathered outside my room every morning for "darshan," some of them even coming from other villages for a glimpse of this "American sadhu." After several days I decided, though with great reluctance, that the time had come for me to depart.

Sri Rama Yogi seems to have a special love for me. And I myself, certainly, feel deep, deep love for him. He told me, "You have good samskars. That is why I have discussed these points with you. Otherwise, as people will tell you, I rarely speak of these deeper matters."

He added, "From the questions you've put, I see that you know more about spiritual truth than any of those numerous sadhus who go about the country lecturing. You have nothing to fear from any challenges they put to you." He said also that he would love to visit me in my ashram in Delhi, if I am able to get it going. [My attempt to found an ashram there, though pursued with Daya Mata's consent and approval, became the cause, later, of the greatest tragedy of my life. She and the SRF Board of Directors cast me out of SRF "on my ear," as I have put it, for what they described (to me, unbelievably) as my insubordination, disobedience, egotism, and treachery. Here, however, is not the place to describe that deeply unhappy period of my life.]

Before departing, I offered Sri Rama Yogi a silver cup, which someone had given me in Sicily. He declined to accept it, stating with a sweet smile, "All I want is your love." He then went into his room and returned with another silver cup, and a spoon, also of silver, which, he told me, he had used for many years. He also gave me a flashlight.

"These are merely symbols," he said sweetly. At this point I insisted that he accept my own proffered gift of my silver cup, and this time he couldn't refuse it! He gazed long and steadily into my eyes, flooding my being with great love and peace. Oh! How difficult I found it to tear myself away!

That evening I addressed the V.R. College in Nellore, where Professor Rao is a lecturer in the Botany department. I spoke on Master and his mission. The college plans to put up a portrait of Babaji, and may also put up one of Master.

Incidentally, while I was in the ashram I was shown a letter from Lou Blevins [one of our SRF monks in Encinitas]. Lou seems to be planning to write a book, and wants Sri Rama Yogi to share his impressions of Master and of Master's visit to Ramanashram in 1936. Lou is incorrigibly curious! The first time he wrote in this vein, Yogi Ramiah didn't reply. Now Lou has repeated his request. Swamiji doesn't want to reply cuttingly, but he feels the question is not proper. Shall he tell Lou that Paramhansaji was a great yogi? Doesn't Lou have enough faith in his guru to know already that he is great? Lou's question, Swamiji feels, is not prompted by a genuine desire for understanding.

Another incidental point: If you yourself, Daya Ma, think of going to that ashram on your next visit to India, be prepared for the most primitive toilet facilities yet: an open-spaced area, partly concealed by a low brick wall on one side, and a flat, muddy expanse of bare ground with a wooden plank stretching out over it. The place isn't cleaned daily, either—nor even every two days! I definitely felt a need to keep on affirming, "I have no likes and dislikes!" For you, this single obstacle would be even more of a problem.

Well, I've taken up a lot of your time. Let me now close.

In Master's love,

ℰↄ ℰↄ ℰↄ ℰↄ ℰↄ ℰↄ ℰↄ ℰↄ

Afterthoughts

Several questions may occur to the reader, upon reading the above letter. I shall try to anticipate them with what follows.

1. Sri Rama Yogi (Yogi Ramiah) had two gurus. Which one of them was the *satguru*, or true teacher, and why couldn't he have been helped by the first one even though he was no longer in the body? I would say, first of all, that Ramana Maharshi was his *satguru*. Yet it is noteworthy that Yogi Ramiah had already attained that supreme state in which "knowing, knower, and known" are (as Master put it in his great poem, "Samadhi") perceived as one. So am I right? Possibly not. Certainly, Yogi Ramiah stated as the best practice something that I believe Ramana Maharshi himself didn't recommend. The Maharshi used to tell people to concentrate in the heart, rather

than at the point between the eyebrows (as Master recommended, and as is recommended in the Bhagavad Gita).

Can the guru continue to help his disciple when he is no longer in the body? Master told us he would do so. I do not know why Yogi Ramiah needed to go to another for clarification on the point he asked about. He was highly evolved enough, in fact, not really to need a guru at all. He seems to have had that consciousness already before coming to Ramana Maharshi. So—I guess we just have to accept the story as it was told, and be satisfied that we have our own path to God.

Master did once tell me, however, that the disciple must have "at least one physical contact with the guru." One disciple insisted it didn't mean necessarily in the present life, but to me this is unsatisfactory, for it depends too much on blind belief. I think what Master meant was that he would continue to guide *through his disciples* those who came to him for help.

2. Master said, "Those who continue to the end will be received into the other world by me or by one of the other gurus." He added, however, that he wasn't referring to those who "merely stuck it out to the end." It was necessary, in other words, to develop inwardly through one's outer service. The important thing, for every devotee, is to turn his karmic service inward, that it continue all his life to free him from ego-consciousness, and to expand his identity with a broader reality (which includes the feelings and realities of others).

3. I took Sri Rama Yogi's words about executive activity to mean that it, too, must be performed without egoic involvement (if it is to be self-liberating), and with ever-increasing sympathy and concern for others. To view executive responsibilities as important *in themselves* is to prolong one's bondage to delusion.

4. The story of the man sent out to care for the cows implies a level of faith in the guru that requires also deep intuition on the disciple's

part, strongly supported by a society that insists on the need for a true guru. For, certainly, the guru in the story put his disciple through a series of tests comparable to those endured centuries ago by Tibet's great yogi Milarepa. One asks, Didn't the ashram itself benefit from the milk that those cows gave? and from the fruit hang- ing from those trees? This is a story in which one has to imagine a very heavy karma on the disciple's part, and an extraordinary motivation (such as Milarepa had) for accepting those tests with an even mind—indeed, amazingly, with good cheer. Otherwise, one must simply accept the story as valid "in principle," which indeed it is. For the disciple who obeys his guru *implicitly*, satisfied that the guru has the spiritual realization to take him to God, is the one who will reach the goal.

In my own life, I was divided in my heart between the desire to devote myself to a life of service, and a conflicting one: to be a solitary hermit. Master told me my life would be one of outer service primar-ily, and I was obedient to his instructions even though times came when I envied those who could give all their energy to meditation. Still, I have seen that the most important thing has been to develop an inner *consciousness* of absorption in God. Thus, I have always kept, as my bottom line, a determination to make my peace of mind my priority. If ever that has been threatened, I have relinquished the activity itself rather than continue with my outward, apparent duty.

5. In the story of the disciple who hauled wood for the ashram, we must assume that, while he carried the wood, he kept his mind on God and on the joy within. Otherwise, he would not have grown nearly so much, spiritually, for he would only have been expiating karma. The best karma cannot give one God. Liberation comes from attunement with the guru's state of consciousness, and by God's grace.

6. It is important, therefore, as Sri Rama Yogi said, and as Mas-ter often counseled us, to be primarily inward in any work we do for

God and Guru. The more we deepen our attunement, even during activity, the better we can serve their cause.

7. To ask, "Who am I?" is the method of self-inquiry recommended by Ramana Maharshi. Sri Rama Yogi implied that every devotee must pursue the same line of inquiry. That line can be pursued in more than one way, however. To feel that God is the doer in all our activities is one important way Master recommended. To focus on infinity, as in Master's suggestion that we learn and recite his poem, *Samadhi*, daily, is also important. To seek to expand our consciousness by universal sympathy and identity is another method. The most important thing is, by attunement with the guru, to try to absorb into one's self his vast state of consciousness.

8. Sri Rama Yogi's statement that disciples often miss the true import of their gurus' teachings deserves constant, humble recognition and reflection.

9. His advice to concentrate on only one chakra must be balanced against those techniques of yoga which recommend focusing progressively on the different chakras. Kriya Yoga does this. Sri Rama Yogi's counsel was less directed toward the yoga science as a whole than toward the focus one should have when he is not practicing the yoga techniques, but is simply meditating.

Master once told me, "Concentrate more in the heart." This was valid for that particular period of my sadhana, but I see Rama Yogi's emphasis as being generally right and important. The energy of loving devotion in the heart can easily be drawn downward, or outward. It is not so, when that energy is directed upward. And it is not so when the entire focus is on the spiritual eye, absorbing all one's devotion at that point.

10. The spiritual influences of food are very important. Hence also the value of our Spirit-in-Nature flower essences.

11. Hong-Sau practice can effectively honor the precept not to divide one's concentration if one concentrates on the flow of breath *at the point of its entry* into the body, which is at the *source* of the nose, very close to the point between the eyebrows. "Hong," a *bij mantra*, gathers ego, the thought of "I," and dissolves it in "Saha," the Infinite Consciousness.

12. In the AUM technique, one should gradually bring one's attention to the right ear, primarily, letting one's chant at the point between the eyebrows become more automatic. Later, however, as the sound becomes strong, one should let what he hears in the right ear be heard also in the left ear. He should then direct it, as before, to the Kutastha center in the forehead.

Part II
LETTERS FROM INDIA

❋ Preface ❋

INDIA — SYMBOL FOR WESTERNERS of mystery, of compelling beauty, of spiritual inspiration! The genius of India's civilization is its fascination with the call of the Infinite to the soul of man. Like the legends of Lord Krishna, ever enticing devotees away from worldliness with the haunting melodies of his flute, India calls to us to leave our preoccupation with brief, worldly life, and to seek the freedom and joy of Spirit.

Swami Kriyananda offers us something of rare value in this book. His account, though deeply personal, transcends mere individual experience in a vision of India's universal—and, to most visitors, so elusive!—spirit.

These letters were written by Kriyananda to devotees in America during his trip to India in the winter of 1972–73. They describe with profound insight, sparkling humor, and, most of all, with deep love and respect, the richness of Indian life—her people, her great saints, her culture, her religion. Through Swamiji's eyes a vivid picture emerges which captures this great land in a timeless pose. In him India has found a son who can hear her elusive melodies, and sing them in such a way that others, too, may hear them.

❊ Introduction ❊

Ananda Cooperative Village
Nevada City, California
May 1973

THIS IS THE STORY of a spiritual journey—in most ways, a deeply personal pilgrimage. Yet it has become a journey and a pilgrimage also for increasing numbers of truth-seekers today. For them, and for others too who may at least have wondered about the magical lure of India, this account of my recent experiences may help to inspire and instruct—and, yes, perhaps also to soften an element of shock that awaits many Westerners on their first exposure to that ancient, incredibly complex civilization.

I don't believe anyone can really understand a nation, or for that matter another human being, unless his understanding is rooted in love. And even at that I doubt that his insights will be worth sharing unless they are based on a familiarity of several years—or, failing in that, on an acquaintance of less than one week.

Does this last alternative sound flippant? First impressions often do penetrate straight to the heart of things. And even if later they turn out to have been mistaken, they usually manage at least to remain interesting. Thirteen years ago, on the strength of a single day spent in Galilee, I got an article accepted by the Jerusalem Post. Had I remained there a year, I wonder if I would have found as much to say.

For after a week in a country (or a month, or however long it takes for first impressions to be blunted by the prosaic cycle of daily living), one finds it increasingly difficult to be clear in his opinions. For one thing, he faces the ineluctable fact that the world is not so radically different from one place to another: It is the same earth, the same sky, the same combinations of elements. People, too, are not nearly so much Frenchmen or Indians or Americans as they are human beings, with the universal needs of mankind: love, happiness, security, understanding. For another, even the superficial differences present, on familiarity, such a tangle of contradictions that it becomes almost impossible to sort them out into neat patterns. Once the veneer of novelty wears off, many years may pass before one attains that level of perspective where complexity resolves itself once again in fundamental simplicity.

In no country on earth are inherent self-contradictions more numerous than in India. Hers is the world's oldest continuous civilization. Countless, varied elements have combined toward making her what she is today. India also betrays that lofty disdain for consistency which one often finds in elderly people, to whom organization, competition, and efficiency seem but symptomatic of the lamentable madness of youth.

My love affair with India began nearly twenty-five years ago, in 1948. The actual contact was physically distant, yet spiritually more immediate than it could possibly have been had I gone there straight off, a total stranger, and roamed about her streets and villages, seeing sights, viewing views, and meeting people in the vague hope of somehow capturing her essence. As a circle is determined by its center, so a nation evolves out of the central attitudes that it holds towards life and the universe. India's true genius — more so than that of any other civilization on earth — has always been her spiritual insight. It was this genius which I touched on first, when, in 1948, I met my Guru, the great Master-yogi, Paramhansa Yogananda, surely the greatest ambassador ever to come out of India. From him I learned about the *true* India—not the India of shifting social customs, of frequent political unrest, but the timeless abode of great sages and of ardent lovers of God. I entered my Guru's ashram as a monk, and for the next ten years immersed myself in his simple, but thrillingly profound explanations of India's ancient teachings.

Destiny beckoned me to India almost from the first. I had been with him less than six months when, one day, looking at me with a quiet smile, he said, "I have plans for you." I knew at once that he was thinking of sending me to India, and at first I was overjoyed. Then suddenly the realization struck me that this would mean leaving him. *He* was my India! To me, always, the two have remained inextricably one. To my relief I then learned that he too was planning to go. For three years in a row, out of compassion for his many devotees in India, he tried to make the journey. But it was not to be, and I see now, from quiet hints he dropped, that he had always known it. As he often did, he was only directing our future thoughts—bending a few twigs to help the branches to grow the way he wanted them to. The last year that we planned to go was 1952, the year he left his body.

For the next six years I continued to serve in Self-Realization Fellowship, the international organization which he had founded, and to wait for the opportunity, always expected, to visit India.

This opportunity came at last in 1958. For the better part of the next four years I lived in India, visiting saints, meeting the people, and absorbing ancient, subtle vibrations. I also lectured around the country on behalf of our local affiliate, Yogoda Satsanga Society, and generally helped with the affairs of that organization. Among the saints with whom I spent considerable time in various parts of

India was one whom I got to meet again on my recent visit: Ma Anandamayee, the "Joy-permeated Mother."

During my years there I did get south a few times—to Bombay, Madras, Pondicherry, Kodaicanal, and Nellore—but most of my time was spent in the north and northeast of India: Calcutta, Ranchi, Delhi, Punjab, and various parts of the Himalayas (including a cave on the banks of the Ganges) where I went occasionally for periods of seclusion and meditation.

Now, if I were to finish by stating simply that I returned to America in 1962, and after ten years visited India again, the reader would be given no insight into much of the reason why this recent visit was so particularly meaningful and important to me. If I'm going to do more than drag you along with me in the impersonal capacity of a tour guide, I think I had better touch on certain experiences of mine which, though not usual material for an introduction of this sort, will at the same time help you really to travel with me as a friend, and to experience India through my eyes.

As a lecturer I became fairly well known in northern India, especially around New Delhi, where I started a meditation center and for some time held regular weekly worship services. As many as 2,000 people at a time attended my public lectures. At one yoga class series about 1,700 people enrolled. Because the response was so good I set out, with the approval of our society's president, Sri Daya Mata, to found a Yogoda ashram in New Delhi. Considerable public interest was awakened in the project, to the extent that Prime Minister Jawaharlal Nehru himself decided to waive a ruling against granting land in the area designated as "green belt." With his personal blessings, we were given the authorization to develop twenty-five acres of this choice land—and not in an area far outside the city, where most of the green belt is situated, but close to Connaught Circus, the very heart of New Delhi.

It was no small triumph. Over 2,000 other societies had already tried to get land anywhere that they could in the green belt. Every one of them so far had been refused.

Miraculously successful though our project seemed, however, it was after all destined not to be. While all my concentration had been directed toward winning the approval of the Indian Government, it hadn't occurred to me that there might be objections to the venture from my own associates in America. Our president had, of course, approved my basic plan, but even she was not expecting anything quite so venturesome as this. I tried to point out to my fellow Board members that nothing less bold could possibly have won the government's approval; the whole venture would simply have failed. But alas, the very boldness of my plans looked to my co-workers in America as though I were planning to undermine the already-established centers of our work in Ranchi and Calcutta.

There followed a painful period for everyone concerned. I still believe we would have cut twenty years off our efforts to develop the work in India had my plan been accepted, but I made the mistake of trying to justify my own personal motives instead of impersonally pleading for the validity of the plan itself.

It is easier to understand things in retrospect. The truth is, anyone in an organization who dares repeatedly to attempt the impossible, even though from the purest desire to serve, will always be viewed as potentially a threat to the stability of the institution. For fourteen years my enthusiasm had been encouraged; I had repeatedly been given positions of responsibility, including at last that of international vice president of SRF/YSS. But there was always that uneasy feeling: "What on earth will he come up with *next?*" The Delhi project finally weighted the balance in my disfavor. People decided that obviously, after all, my enthusiasm could never have been anything but insubordination of the worst kind. To tolerate it any longer would be to endanger the very work itself.

Some people there are who, perhaps too innately eccentric, don't seem cut out for organizational work. Perhaps I am one of them. At any rate, matters deteriorated for me from this time onwards. Whatever I did now to go on serving the work, my every gesture seemed to threaten nameless menace. It was, to be sure, my own karma; I blame no one but myself. Indeed, the bond of love that I share with my fellow disciples is so deep that this whole difficult episode has not substantially affected it.

In the end, a cablegram summoned me to New York City. There I was asked to resign from the Board of Directors and the vice presidency of SRF/YSS, and was informed that the organization had no further need of my disservices.

I was now on my own, and in need of finding some way whereby I could continue to seek God through service to my Guru. For a time I thought I might return to India and live in seclusion in the Himalayas. But when bad karma descends, it often does so with a vengeance. Someone (SRF definitely disclaims responsibility for the deed[*]) had reported to the Indian Government that I was an American spy, and also (horror of horrors!) a Christian missionary in disguise. From one angle it is amusing, but the practical outcome of the accusations was that I was denied a visa. Repeatedly through the years I tried to return; always permission was refused me.

In retrospect, I see that I had certain works to do that could not have been done either in a large organization or in India. It was during this period that I fulfilled a dream that Master (as I usually refer to my Guru) always held dear: the founding of a yoga-oriented, cooperative village. It is called Ananda Cooperative Village, and is

---

[*] In fact, at the time Swami Kriyananda was writing, he already had proof that SRF/YSS was responsible, but in this book he chose not to present it. —Publisher's note

situated on 350 acres of land in the beautiful foothills of the Sierra Nevada mountains. Here, nearly 100 devotees live and serve God.*

During this period also I did the research for, and wrote a book on the crisis of meaning: *Crises in Modern Thought*,† a vitally important work—at least for me, since it discharges a responsibility. I have felt to do what I can to answer in its own terms the often-heard charge that everything is meaningless.

At last, in August of 1972, I heard from the Indian Government that they were willing to let me return to New Delhi and plead my case in person. I arranged to leave last November. (Interestingly, the very day before my departure from Ananda I received the first advance copies of *Crises in Modern Thought*. My obligations had been discharged. I was free now to return to my Guru's country, my spiritual motherland.)

I left San Francisco on November 12 for London, where I spent just enough time to talk to a few publishers about handling my books, and to have an evening *satsang* (spiritual gathering) with a few devotees at Centre House, where I was staying. From London I flew to Rome, where I had been invited by several friends. On November 22 I flew on to India.

My total time in India was only a little over two months. But in the light of what I have said earlier in these pages, the brevity of this visit made it doubly interesting, for the immediacy of first impressions was preserved, though tempered by the slower, deeper rhythms of an old friendship.

---

* I've related the story of my separation from SRF, and the building of Ananda, in my book *A Place Called Ananda*. In the years since this book was first published, Ananda (now known as Ananda World Brotherhood Community) has flourished on all levels. —SK, 2007 [Later retitled by the author *Go On Alone: A Struggle Between Personal Integrity and the Demand for Conformity.* —Publisher's note]

† Many years later I revised the book extensively, and renamed it *Out of the Labyrinth: For Those Who Want to Believe, But Can't.* —SK, 2007

What follows is mostly excerpts from letters that I wrote to the members of our Ananda community. Wherever necessary or helpful, however, I have added comments and explanations that would help to give the reader a fuller picture of the matters under discussion. And, with apologies to the persons concerned, I have omitted most of the names of friends, both old and new, whom I encountered on the journey. For in too many a diary of this nature one gets the impression that the writer was more intent on tossing bouquets to the people he had met on his journey than on instructing the general reader.

CHAPTER ONE

❋ Christian Shrines ❋

Rome
November 22, 1972

Dear Ones:

Here I am, finally ready to leave for Bombay this afternoon. The trip has been pleasant. Even the weather in London was beautiful, which for London is saying a lot; it stayed that way throughout my visit.

In London I saw several publishers, one or two of whom at least seemed interested in publishing my books. I had one *satsang* (spiritual gathering), and visited Mrs. Gertrude White, the longtime center leader for Self-Realization Fellowship, and a friend of mine since 1955. I also had an opportunity to visit a childhood friend of mine, Joan Hart; it was the first time we had seen each other since prewar days in Romania! And I had a happy stay at Centre House, where I made a number of new friends.

And then, almost before I knew it, I was up in the skies again and headed for Rome. It was friends of mine here who had made it possible for me to visit Europe. (This whole trip, in fact, has been a present from several generous friends.)

My visit to Italy has been hectic, but interesting, and blessed with occasional periods of real inspiration. I visited the Sistine Chapel, and spent a day at Assisi, the town of Saint Francis, meditating in many of the places associated with his life.

Master (Paramhansa Yogananda) used to refer to Saint Francis as his patron saint. He loved him more than any of the other Christian saints, for his joy and childlike simplicity. I, too, have found enormous inspiration from this beautiful saint. But reading about him is a very different kind of inspiration from actually visiting the places where he lived, and where his vibrations are still a powerful, living force.

I was not prepared to feel in his presence such a wonderful sweetness as I experienced when, sitting in meditation at Rivotorto, and again at the Porziuncola, his blessings filled my soul. And then I understood anew the value of pilgrimage: not going places only to *see*, but above all inwardly to commune. It is for this kind of inner contact, above all, that I am going to India.

Feeling the divine sweetness of Saint Francis in my meditation, I wondered: How is it possible for anyone to be so utterly sweet? And then the answer came: By never judging anyone; by being from one's heart a brother or a sister to all; by complete humility — but above all by never judging. I think this virtue can be perfected only by keeping one's thoughts always fixed, as Saint Francis kept his, on God! God! God!*

Saint Francis was, we are assured, "a true son of the church." Indeed, his obedience and loyalty never seem to have faltered. Yet he was certainly not a "true" son in the sense of being a "chip off the old block." The Church would never have set out deliberately to produce such progeny. Finding itself unexpectedly blessed with such an offspring, it did its best to remold Francis in its own image. No one could have been less attuned to the way in which the Church saw itself, which I suppose is the safest way of judging what the Church

---

* Saint Francis once came to Paramhansa Yogananda in a vision, and gave him the beautiful poem, "God! God! God!" I have set this poem to music. It is my hope someday to record it. [I finally did record it — thirty years later! — on my album *I've Passed My Life as a Stranger, Lord.* —SK, 2007]

really was. The Church saw itself as a powerful institution: Francis wanted to turn people away from the institutionalized aspects of religion; he didn't even want his disciples to construct buildings to live in. The Church sought to guide its flock by legislation; Francis supported the laws of the Church, but urged people to seek their guidance more from God, inwardly. The Church was concerned with ruling over its flock; Francis was concerned only with sharing his joy with people. It was not that the two, Saint Francis and the Church, held views that were mutually exclusive. Each in a sense complemented the other. But each saw reality as if through opposite ends of the telescope.

I got a glimpse of this contrast the other day, when I visited the Vatican museum. This place is filled, it is true, with great works of art. It must be mostly my own shortcoming that I wasn't able to enjoy them as much as I might have in a different setting. For somehow the thought of all that concentration of opulence and beauty in a place devoted to religious guidance reminded me of that paradox, which I had just finished writing into my new book, *Eastern Thoughts, Western Thoughts*: first, the common expectation, "The greater the worldly power, the greater the power to do good"; and then the common discovery, "The greater the worldly power, the smaller the *desire* to do good."

The Sistine Chapel is described cosily as "the Pope's private chapel," but is large enough for a congregation of considerable size, and was more than large enough to accommodate what I suppose is the usual huge throng of visitors. It contains some of the greatest paintings in the world — a fact which doesn't exactly help to guarantee the Pope his privacy. Of course, I loved the paintings.

If one goes to the Sistine Chapel hoping for spiritual inspiration, however, he may be disappointed. The inspiration of these paintings is more on an artistic level. Seeing Michelangelo's painting of the Last Judgment, the thought occurred to me that, while the damned looked properly damned all right—sufficiently so to satisfy the most vindictive (though, of course, ever-loving!) Father—the elect didn't look too happy over their good fortune. I detected no joy in their faces, nor in the attitudes of their bodies. The sum of their "bliss" seemed to be the fact that at least *they* weren't being physically tortured.

It was as though all the energy in the painting had been directed towards punishing the poor damned. And that, I thought, is what too much of traditional religion has done in concentrating so much on sin. The joys of salvation, in this view, seem almost negative—a mere reprieve from absolute and well-deserved misery.

It hasn't been altogether a restful holiday so far. Those last weeks at Ananda, when I worked past midnight every night to finish off all my pending projects, put me in need of a little rest. Or so I thought, but God seems to have thought otherwise. I've had many interviews, and much activity. But it has been very nice seeing old friends again, and meeting new ones.

Some of these friends are raising the difference in fare to bring me back by way of Rome, instead of flying on across the Pacific. So I'll be here again next February.

It was wonderful seeing so many of you at the San Francisco airport. What a sweet memory to carry with me on my journey! In not very many places in this world can one find such a concentration of beautiful souls. People on this journey, in looking at my photographs of Ananda, constantly remark on your happy, shining faces.

I tried writing you all a letter in my inimitable handwriting. And then I thought, Do they deserve such cruel punishment? Their karma can't be so bad! So I bought this little Olivetti "Lettera 32" with some money a friend here had given me for my expenses in Rome.

Must rush now. I'm being picked up in a few minutes and haven't finished packing yet. Come to think of it, I haven't even started!

With love always in God,

CHAPTER TWO

❋ India—First Impressions ❋

Bombay
November 24, 1972

Here I am at last—my first visit to India in over ten years.

The flight from Rome was something special: first class accommodations, which Alitalia seems to go out of its way to make really *swank*. I still had only my economy class ticket, but the flight captain was a friend of a friend of a friend of mine, and somehow, this tenuous link was enough to win me special favors. Even so, I got only two hours' sleep. I think it will take me several days now really to recuperate.

I witnessed something strange and tragic at the airport in Rome. There had been a strike of porters, and people had to carry all their own luggage onto and off the planes. It was pitiable to see little women and old people forced to drag heavy suitcases down hundred-yard corridors. In America the strong would automatically have helped the weak, but in Rome nobody that I saw did anything to help anybody. I remarked to a friend, "What if some little old lady in her eighties is forced to carry her own bags? She may easily die of a heart attack!" Hardly two minutes later I heard cries of, "Oh! Oh!" An elderly man had just dropped his bags and was swaying back and forth. A moment later he staggered backward and fell to the floor. Two or three doctors among the passengers tried to revive him. Of the airport personnel there wasn't a sign for the next fifteen or twenty minutes. Five or ten minutes passed, then the man again cried, "Oh! Oh!" A few moments later, he expired. All that the airport personnel could do when they arrived was cover him with a sheet. I was there another hour or so, and they still hadn't gotten around to removing him.

How strange is karma! Here was this poor man, possibly on an eagerly awaited vacation, dying unattended, more alone in a crowd than he would have been in his own bedroom. I hope my prayers for him eased his passing. But how uncertain is human life. This was the first time I had ever seen anyone die (except when my Guru left his body, but that never struck me as death). The very indignity of this scene underscored for me how essentially alone man is. A lifetime of struggle, ambition, and rewards; of friends and possessions gathered lovingly around him as if to form a hedge of security against the all-devouring void: and suddenly a callous slap from death, and out he soars—alone yet once again, his securities and fulfillments scattered like dust in a hurricane. Death is important to life. It is an essential prod to us to shun human pettiness, and to seek the only true Friend we have ever had: God.

(May 1973: In India, later, I was told that to see a corpse is a good omen. Who would have thought it so! Then I remembered having seen a dead man—my first glimpse of death in this life—in an auto accident on my way across America in 1948 to meet my Guru. In some ways, this last trip to my Guru's country held a similar meaning for me: the end of an old chapter in my spiritual life, and the beginning of a new one.)

Bombay has grown incredibly in the eleven years since I last saw it; from three million inhabitants to nearly six million. The crowds are everywhere. So also is the noise. In a taxi, stern non-attachment seems to be the only possible way to avoid a heart attack. The taxi driver, relying on God and on his horn with a faith that, under other circumstances, might be inspiring, beeps and bullies his way through a veritable sea of pedestrians, bicycles, cattle, hand-drawn carts, lorries, and motor scooters, all of them seemingly headed in different directions at vastly different speeds. The unspoken rule of the road is, "Might is right." A crowd of pedestrians will be crossing at an intersection. (In a few areas, pedestrians do seem to have learned to obey this basic principle of traffic safety.) Incredibly, the taxi driver actually speeds up as he approaches them, relying on God's gift to him of a horn to scatter them in time to prevent a major disaster.

Bombay has never been my favorite Indian city. More efficient than most, it yet lacks the spiritual vibrations of the India I love. Everything here is business, worldly ambition, greed, self-gratification. As I walk down Mahatma Gandhi Road (was ever a street more inappropriately named?), I am approached every five or ten steps: "Wanna change money? I buy dollars, good price." "No," I say, "I am here because I love India. I don't want to hurt her." Most money changers quickly give up, turning away to seek new prospects. But one of them thanks me gently. "You see, sir," he explains, "we are too poor to be honest. But we appreciate it when we meet honest people like your good self." He proceeds to walk many blocks to help me find a place I've been looking for. His is a sad commentary on India's present frame of mind—transitional, morally and spiritually confused as it leaves the relative stability of the past and gropes its way toward new ways of handling old problems of poverty and overpopulation.

I've been told much about the increasing corruption and greed in India. It will be interesting to see what my own reactions are. Still, I haven't come here to study India's social problems. My immediate goal is the ashram of one of her living saints.

Swami Muktananda visited us at Ananda two years ago, and was kind enough to promise to help me with my visa problem. He invited me to come and stay in his ashram. Right now I am visiting the home of one of his chief disciples, "Papa" Trivedi, a wealthy man who devotes his entire life to serving his guru. Also staying with his family is Uma Berliner, an American disciple of Baba's (as Muktananda is generally called) who has come to Bombay for a couple of days to see printers in connection with the ashram magazine, of which she is the editor. Uma already looks more Indian than American, but her strong New York accent gives her away. She helps to prepare me for things to expect at the ashram. And Papa tells many stories culled from his years with Baba. One amusing one I'll share with you.

They had been traveling somewhere in India, and came to a remote village where they put up for the night in a government rest house. There was no electricity in the village. As it grew dark, one candle was lit in each room; this was the full extent of their illumination. A late visitor, the local schoolmaster, complained that he couldn't see Baba.

Suddenly the whole room became flooded with light. The visitor, terrified by this display of yogic power, fled without even looking at the man he had complained he couldn't see.

"Baba used sometimes to do things like that," Papa Trivedi told me, "just for fun."

Papa is also the man through whom Swami Muktananda intends to get my visa problem straightened out. He seems to know just about everyone at the top levels of government. On his advice, I have written a letter to the Home Ministry in New Delhi. Now we'll see what develops.

In the meantime, my short interlude in Bombay is running out. I'm scheduled to leave with Papa tomorrow morning for Muktananda's ashram at Ganeshpuri.

Chapter Three

❋ Swami Muktananda ❋

Ganeshpuri
November 29, 1972

I'm writing this from Swami Muktananda's ashram. We drove over miles of dry, not very populated countryside to get here. Suddenly, far off to the left of us, Uma pointed out Shree Gurudev Ashram, as this is called, rising high above the plain in a rich oasis of trees. Soon we had parked the car. Fending off a crowd of children begging (Uma told me Baba doesn't want people to encourage them by giving them anything; they all have families, and none of them is really poor), we entered the ashram gates. I waited around for Baba to appear. In the meantime I was warmly greeted by Amma and Professor Jain, disciples of Baba's who had come with him to America. (Amma, as it happens, is also Papa Trivedi's sister.) They told me Baba had been asking after me.

At last Baba came out. I went over and made my *pronam* (bow) to him.

"Why didn't you come sooner?" he inquired. "I was expecting you two weeks ago."

"I'm sorry, Baba. I couldn't get away any sooner, and then I was invited to stop over in Europe on the way."

"Good, it's good you have come." After a few minutes he told me to go down to the "cave" (a basement room in the main building) and meditate.

Later I was shown to my quarters. I had been told to expect the red carpet treatment. This turned out to mean a room in a special building reserved for visiting *sadhus* (holy men), at some distance from the main hub of activity. It has a perfectly lovely garden in front of it, giving it really the appearance of a sort of Shangri-La. Neat walks are hedged with colorful bougainvillea and shaded by spreading trees.

Alas, nothing in this relative universe is ever completely perfect. A very loud loudspeaker "graces" the roof just above my window. Tape recordings are blasted over it several times daily for the inspiration of the entire countryside. There is also a huge kettle drum very near my window, almost large enough to lie down on; it is used to accompany *arati* (a devotional service), and for announcing "lights out" in the evening. The loudspeaker blesses us with recorded chanting from 3:30 to 4:30 every morning. The kettle drum joins in exuberantly for the last fifteen or twenty minutes of this, creating what feels like a minor cataclysm.

The chanting here is of a style different from what I am accustomed to. For one thing, it is very loud, and set to melodies that, I'm afraid, don't really appeal to me. The devotees are obviously sincere, and get a lot from their style of singing even if I don't, so maybe it is my fault for not tuning in properly.

This must surely be one of the most beautiful ashrams in India. The devotees work hard to keep the grounds lovely. There are about a hundred people living here, some two thirds of them Westerners, and a very nice group they are.

Baba is visited by an endless stream of pilgrims — hundreds of them every day. So far I've had no chance to speak with him alone. All one can do is stand in line for his blessings, murmur a hasty word, then back off to make room for the next person. We had a very enjoyable question-and-answer session yesterday, so one can get at least some of one's questions aired that way. But in fact, I haven't much to ask him except perhaps about my own *sadhana* (spiritual practice). Master (my Guru) gave me enough spiritual teachings to answer almost any conceivable question that I might have.

The main thing I am here for is a chance to deepen my own meditations. These are getting better, but I'm still recuperating from overwork those last weeks at Ananda, plus the normal fatigue of long-distance travel, with all those sudden time changes.

One difficulty I'm facing is that a certain few of the devotees here insist that I should join them in their six hours of daily chanting. I've told them that I'm here not to learn their form of *sadhana*, but to deepen my own. After twenty-four years on the path, I feel no need for a new approach to God. All I'm looking for is a chance to concentrate more one-pointedly on my own, Guru-given approach, relieved as I am for a time from the burdens of daily work and responsibility. Really, I should think it obvious that it would be wasting my precious time here to try to adjust myself to unfamiliar practices, considering that I'll only have to leave them anyway in a few weeks—perhaps just as I'm beginning to grow accustomed to them. But I'm afraid my decision has been interpreted by certain devotees here as a rejection of their way of life. A couple of them have even called my apparent aloofness "insulting." I was most surprised. At Ananda we encourage guests to meditate, whatever their style of meditation. Anyone, whatever his path, who devotes all his time in trying to deepen his contact with God is considered by us a blessing on the community, not an insult. I've told these good people that their pressure on me to conform to their routine could make the difference between whether I stay or leave.

But Professor Jain tells me to ignore them. "Baba has told you to do what you are doing. That is enough." I certainly hope so. Yet I admit I'm uncomfortable. I don't think it good for a guest ever to be an offense to anyone, no matter who it is that supports him. Professor Jain considers my delicacy on this point misplaced on the spiritual path. Of course I see his point. This world, after all, is only a dream; we should not play its games, but one-pointedly seek to gain whatever insights we can into Ultimate Reality, and move quietly forward toward our own salvation. Yet the fact is, I am simply not capable, even for the best of reasons, of ignoring others' feelings while I "get mine." This somewhat callous attitude, definitely favored here in the name of firmness of resolution, predicates a measure of indifference to the feelings of others that would be impossible in one who has devoted his life to serving people. Dispassion is not the same thing as indifference. To me, firmness in the face of opposition is a virtue only when the issues involved are impersonal, which in this case they are not.

By the way, Professor Jain says Baba considers Ananda the best ashram in America. A number of the people here have expressed a desire to visit us. On the whole, as I said, everyone has been most friendly to me.

Ganeshpuri
December 10, 1972

I went to Bombay the other day to take care of a few things. While there I became quite sick. But on the whole my health has been fine.

I've had a couple of private talks lately with Baba, mostly on matters pertaining to my own meditations. But I'm learning that what God wants me to gain from my visit to India this time is not advice from this person or from that, but rather a deeper inspiration from my own inner Self. Muktananda himself said, "It is easy to see just from looking at you that you are one who is centered in the

Self." To look to others for help is to seek help outside this Self, when the true answer must ever be to go more within. There is a time, indeed, on the path when outer advice is necessary, but all the advice Baba gave me served only to reinforce my understanding that what I was looking for must be sought within. He himself said so. And perhaps also with this purpose in mind, he challenged my Guru on several points in such a way as to make me cling more firmly than ever to Master's presence in my heart. This is the most priceless gift I have ever received.

I feel it is nearly time for me to depart this ashram. I have a lot of ground still to cover in the short time remaining to me in India.

CHAPTER FOUR

❀ Sayers—Sooth and Unsooth ❀

Delhi
December 20, 1972

I've left the Bombay area. I had planned after leaving Ganeshpuri to go south to Bangalore, there to visit my friend, Sri N. Keshava, and to see the well-known saint, Sri Sathya Sai Baba, then on
to Mangalore to spend Christmas at a well-known ashram called
Anandashram, founded by Swami Ramdas. But I had to change
my plans, as the most important task facing me in India is getting
that visa problem cleared up. Papa Trivedi strongly advised me to
go straight to New Delhi, where a member of parliament whom
Swami Muktananda requested to help me is expected to stay only
until Christmas. Here I have been seeing him, and hope to get the
matter settled soon so that I can go on to visit my best-loved saint,
Ma Anandamayee, in Kanpur, where she will be staying from December 23 to January 8.

The experience at Ganeshpuri proved good for me. It gave me
something I needed. It certainly was not easy; I'm told it never is for
newcomers there. For me, that loudspeaker and drum right outside
my window, the particular style of the chanting, the mathemati-
cally precise rhythm of life at the ashram—and, yes, the fanaticism
of certain of the members—were features to which I never fully
adjusted. But I met some wonderful people there, too, and Baba

81

certainly was loving to me. I came away feeling great inner joy, increased inner depth, and a feeling of Master's constant presence. On the whole, my stay there proved a great blessing for me.

While in Bombay I indulged a couple of whims, and went to see an astrologer whom someone had recommended to me, and a Bhrigu pandit who claims to have ancient records of prediction from which he may be able to read one's personal future. (I encountered two or three Bhrigu pandits on my first visit to India who impressed me with their accuracy. This time I was more interested in gathering data for my account of this strange phenomenon than I was in getting further details on myself.)

The astrologer was quite accurate concerning my past. He said that after my next birthday, on May 19, 1973, all obstacles would be cleared from my path, and that certain sorrows would be lifted at last, but all this only after next May.

This astrologer's English was atrocious. Much of the time I could only barely make out his meaning. But it was also highly amusing. Here are a few excerpts of what he said; I'll repeat them almost verbatim from a recording I made, to give you an idea of unsuspected possibilities latent in the English language.

Astrologer: "From last twelve years period — forty-seven will be complete in May 1973 — what is your ambitions, what is you are thinking from last twelve years, any kind of idea you have got in your mind, you will be successful and you will come out in a real way, in proper way, when will be forty-seven. Why? Saturn is retrograde in your *buddhi*; a very powerful planet Saturn is: exalted. Again also, Rahu [moon's north node] in first house — Rahu is very powerful planet in your horoscope. Rahu, and Mangal [Mars], Guru [Jupiter]. Rahu in first, limit age of forty-two, forty-five, and forty-eight. Rahu's limit is this."

I: "What does that mean?"

Astrologer: "Forty-two, go on. Forty-five, go on. Now forty-eight..."

I: "What do you mean, 'go on'?"

Astrologer: "Go on, go on. Finish. Completed that age. You completed forty-two. You completed forty-five. . . ."

I: "What did I complete?"

Astrologer: "Complete. Now, when will be complete forty-seven, from May 1973, on that time you will come out in the light."

(I finally figured out what he meant. It was that the veils, so to speak, of Rahu's obstruction are lifted one after the other in one's forty-second, forty-fifth, and forty-eighth years. In my own meditations on these matters a year or two ago, I discovered what I believe to be an esoteric connection between Rahu and the upward flowing current of energy through the *ida* nerve channel, as yogis call it, in the spine. This current reflects the upward, life-affirming quality in human nature; also it reinforces this quality. Similarly, the planetary placements at birth reflect, and in turn reinforce, qualities that we've already developed in previous lives. Rahu's obstructions might hinder one's efforts to develop steadiness of purpose; they might reinforce any predisposition to discouragement or lack of drive; they might cause one's enthusiasm to move in spurts rather than in a steady flow. These inner defects would then attract corresponding failures and misfortunes in one's objective life.

(But by strong will power there is no obstacle, whether subjective or objective, that cannot be overcome. As Master used to say: "There are no such things as obstacles. There is only opportunity!")

Astrologer: "Last twelve-years' period you could not got settle, and could not succeed. Now your successful period just going to rise. But you are not going to successful anywhere or any idea or any kind of the job up to age of forty-seven, that means up to May 1973."

(Certainly, whatever little bit I have managed to accomplish in this period of time has been in the face of extraordinary obstacles. Interestingly, it was just twelve years prior to next May, on May 14,

83

1961, that I wrote the report on my activities in New Delhi which brought so much fire onto my head, from America, and which set the direction for all my subsequent activities.)

Astrologer: "No one will be know according your face, but somebody will be know according to your name."

I: "I don't understand."

Astrologer: "Name."

I: "What's this about 'no one will know according to your face'?"

Astrologer: "Face."

I: "What do you mean? Do I look stupid, or something?"

A friend of the astrologer's: "No, you see, what he means is that from your appearance nobody will say that you are an intelligent man. . . ."

Astrologer: (nodding as if with assent) "Your face. Name will be famous, but no one going to know your face, because you won't come out. You going underground—samadhi."

It turned out that what he was trying to say was only that I would be in seclusion, and not in the public eye! But this not until May 1974, when my forty-eighth year will be finished.

Astrologer: "You will be going two country in two place between the May 1973 to '74. You will go another country, you will be remain some time there. Then you will be establishment."

He explained that his predictions of travel were based on my own inner plans or intentions, and therefore amounted to an objective probability.

He was quite accurate for the past, including these words about my childhood: "Even the very childhood—seven, eight years or ten years boy from that time you have got idea I want to go another world; I don't like to remain in this world. World is very happy, and you are thinking world is funny for me; world is good for the others, not for me. That idea you got from the very beginning."

An interesting experience. When I offered to pay him for his time, he refused, then countered by offering me money. When I declined, he gave me a bottle of oil scented with jasmine, and thanked me for having given him so much of my time!

Graciousness is so deeply a part of the Indian character as to be completely unselfconscious. Someone (a Westerner) once told me about a visit he had paid to the city of Jaipur, armed with a letter of introduction to a family there from a friend of his who barely knew them. The family put their home and time completely at his disposal during the two days of his visit. The husband even took those days off from his office to show their guest all the local sights. My acquaintance told me he had quite lost his temper a few days later when another foreigner remarked to him, "Oh, you can't get anywhere with these Indians!"

"Get to know them first," he had replied, "before judging them. You'll soon discover that in your superficial opinions you were only seeing your own self!"

But my experience with the Bhrigu pandit was less impressive. For one thing, money seemed more or less clearly to be his first object. Besides that, I was almost amused at the cheek of the man. First he told me that he would read from only one page, which would apply to me and to no one else. Then, *right in front of me*, he turned to a fresh page for every sentence that he pretended to read out! Moreover, after he had finished reading what he said was all the material he had on me, he asked me whether I had any questions to ask. Dutifully, I asked them. Then he, referring back to "my page" again, pretended to read out a whole group of suddenly materialized answers!

I also saw two or three publishers in Bombay. It would be nice to get my books published in India.

Getting off the plane at New Delhi airport, I was struck anew by the spiritual atmosphere of northern India. Riding on the airport limousine through the night, surrounded by tourists, able to see nothing of the countryside, I yet felt a distinct vibration of joy and soul-freedom such as I have felt from no other place on earth. Truly this is a holy land. The people who inhabit it during this brief span of time are only pilgrims passing through it in a time dimension, as I am passing through it in a space dimension. India can be savored most fully as a thing apart from its temporary scenes. One must withdraw mentally from the noise and the turmoil to feel the silent blessings of countless sages — blessings that still hover over the land as a thrilling call to men to seek eternal values.

So thrilled am I by India's divine atmosphere, here in northern India especially, that I hardly look at the people as I pass through the streets. It is on a more timeless, less nationalistic level that India touches me. When someone asked me recently, "How do you like our country?" I replied, "Well, it is my country, too!"

I've been staying in the home of some old friends of mine, Dr. T.N. Bhan, his wife Rani, and their foster son, Indu. I usually stayed with them whenever I visited Delhi years ago. It is a great joy to renew these old friendships — and not these only, but others in the old circle. Before I leave here, we plan to hold a *satsang* and invite all my old friends. But I'm not in India this time to lecture, so I don't intend to give in to the pressure to see too many people earlier, lest I get drawn into a round of public appearances. Already someone is trying to get me to appear "just once" on the local T.V. station. I've declined.

It's late, but I'll say it again: Have a joyous Christmas!

Chapter Five

❋ The Divine Life Society — Rishikesh ❋

Delhi
December 28, 1972

I should have sent that last letter to you days ago, but — of all crumby excuses — I didn't have an envelope! So I'll enclose it with this one.

I was feeling a bit nostalgic at the thought of missing Christmas completely, so I went to a Christmas party at the U.S. embassy the evening of the 22nd. We sang carols, chatted aimlessly, and people passed in and out, but mostly out. (I'm kidding, of course. There *was* spiked punch for those who wanted it, but it was a thoroughly tame affair — the sort of thing one expects embassies to put on.) The carols were evidently picked with a view to offending no one — Jews, Hindus, atheists, what have you. They were so carefully nonreligious ("Rudolph the Red-Nosed Reindeer," that sort of thing) that they probably succeeded in offending many more people by completely ignoring the true significance of the occasion. For myself, I tried singing a couple of songs, then lost interest. It just wasn't like Christmas at Ananda or in SRF, with that all-day meditation, and those vibrations of Christ's living presence.

Again, I thought, God was telling me, "You've come to India to remind yourself that everything you're seeking is *within*—remember?"

That same evening I took a train to Swami Sivananda's ashram, the Divine Life Society, in Rishikesh. Swami Chidananda, the president of the society, was there. He is one of the monks I respect most in India. He had just returned two days previously from several months in Europe. I had planned to have a quiet time in Rishikesh, keeping mostly to myself, and to consider this my Christmas festivity, but as it turned out, the ashram did Christmas up in a big way, with carols (this time the devotional ones), talks on Jesus, meditation, and general divine festivity. They even had a Christmas tree, and (believe it or not) a blinking neon sign outdoors proclaiming, "MERRY XMAS"! The *satsangs* were really lovely, and satisfied my desire for a touch of the old Christmas spirit. I had to sing and lecture—the price for having had Swami Chidanandaji visit us and lecture at Ananda three years ago. I also had to spend a great deal of time talking to people. In fact, I find it incredible the amount of energy that gets spent here in conversation. I can't get out of it politely. Everyone wants to know about Ananda, or to ask advice, or, if we've met before, to talk about old times. And finally, I got a wretched cold at Rishikesh. But it was worth it. The visit was wonderful, and just what I needed after days of sitting on my hands in Delhi, waiting for news from the Home Ministry.

That visa problem hasn't been fixed up yet. Mr. Raghuramaiah, the member-of-parliament disciple of Swami Muktananda, was to tell me the latest news on Tuesday after my return from Rishikesh, but in the meantime he got called out of town and won't be back until the end of this week. So here I still am, sitting on my hands in a big, worldly city instead of getting to go visit Ma. And there she is, her time in Kanpur slowly running out. Maybe I'll just go there anyway, and let the visa matters hobble along at their own speed without trying to prod them along any faster.

In fact, I'm beginning to suspect that even these delays in Delhi, frustrating as they've seemed to the more spiritual purposes of my journey, have not lacked their own divine purpose. I can't yet explain how, but at least something good seems to be coming of them, inwardly.

Worldly minds don't take too enthusiastically to reports of the unusual things that keep happening in the lives of devotees. "Coincidence" — "sheer luck" — "pious exaggeration": with such words people who lack faith in a Higher Power dismiss every proof of God's loving solicitude for those of His children who place their lives trustingly in His hands.

Perhaps, when talking to worldly people, one ought not to confuse them with too many facts! After all, one doesn't like to take a person's faith away from him — at least, not until he himself seems ready to abandon it for a better one. And the worldly person does have a somewhat primitive kind of "faith": the belief, however pathetic, that human destiny depends entirely on frantic human struggles against Nature's mighty, and all-but-incomprehensible, forces.

But how wonderful is the devotee's life! The more truly he surrenders to God, the more he finds that God really does look after him — even in the insignificant details of daily life. At first the devotee, too (if he is honest), may question whether this or that example of good fortune was not merely a "coincidence." But as the evidence of a loving Providence continues to accumulate, he would be faithless indeed if he continued to seek mundane explanations for every problem that has somehow resolved itself in the best possible way, with a minimum of worrisome effort on his own part. "Take no thought for the morrow," Jesus said. His words deserve to be taken seriously, and literally.

But of course, the kind of faith that most perfectly draws God's help is one which demands every bit as much commitment of one's energy and concentration as the worldly person throws into his strenuous efforts to fend for himself. It won't do to be simply passive. The most obvious difference between the commitment of the devotee and that of the worldly man is, in the devotee, the absence of strain, of thwarting crosscurrents of worry and fear.

It surely was wonderful, within twenty minutes of deciding to go to Rishikesh, to find a berth on that crowded train to Hardwar; to be in Rishikesh (without prior inquiries) at exactly the time when Swami Chidanandaji happened to be there (since I had wanted especially to visit him); and to have my desire fulfilled for some touch of the true, divine Christmas spirit. And at last, on the day when I was to leave Rishikesh, I didn't even make any plans for getting back to Hardwar to meet the Delhi train. I simply felt that, if I left all arrangements in God's hands, He would work out something more spiritually beneficial for me than a long train ride to Hardwar, followed by an afternoon and an evening of sitting around in the railway station waiting for the Delhi train to arrive.

Sure enough, a friend of the Divine Life Society offered—almost at the last possible moment—to drive me to Hardwar, where I spent a delightful afternoon in spiritual discussion with him at his home, and got fed royally.

Some weeks before leaving Ananda Cooperative Village, I read A.J. Cronin's excellent novel, *The Keys of the Kingdom*. It is the story of a priest in China before the war. Parts of the book are inspiring. Yet I was struck by what seemed like a want of divine intervention in the poor priest's life. One would have thought that the sheer law of probability would choose better for him than God did! It isn't that the devotee doesn't get his fair share—and perhaps even more than his share!—of tests and difficulties. But always at least, provided he maintains his faith, he finds in the end that some important lesson has been learned: even in suffering, he discovers God's ever-supportive love; and even in worldly failure, he achieves a higher kind of

Swami Kriyananda visiting Swami Chidananda at the Divine Life Society in Rishikesh in 1995, many years after this book was written.

victory. Poor Father Chisholm! Despite his life of truly heroic dedication to God's service, he was vouchsafed incredibly few signs that God even knew he was alive.

Of course, I suppose a novelist can't afford to tax his readers' credibility too far; he is driven by their ignorance, if not by his own, to be considerably less realistic than reality itself. But, at least on the spiritual path, truth really is (as they say) stranger than fiction.

I remember a trip that I took last summer to Carmel, California, to celebrate the completion of my *Fourteen Lessons in Yoga** (a major undertaking, comparable to a book of some 700 pages). It was in August, at the height of the tourist season. No doubt I should have known better than to visit this major tourist attraction without making advance reservations, but that in fact is what I did. When I arrived at Carmel, I was informed that only a handful of the more

---

* Now titled *The Art and Science of Raja Yoga.*

expensive rooms were available. Directed to the nicest lodge in town, I found they had one room left, and it was expensive.

"Well, Divine Mother," I thought, "there's no turning back now. I'm here to celebrate a job I've just finished for You, so I'll simply hand over to You the problem of *how* to celebrate, too!" I pulled out my wallet to pay for the room. At this point the desk clerk, who had taken a liking to me, stopped me.

"Please," he said, "stay with us as our guest. I'll write you down in the record as a travel agent." I couldn't even talk him out of it!

And I had gone to Carmel dressed in ordinary clothes, not in monastic robes.

Coincidence? The next day I went to a restaurant for lunch, and the owner wouldn't let me pay for my meal!

Again, before I left on this trip I was wondering whether I'd be wandering around London on my own, spending more time and money than I could afford owing to my unfamiliarity with the city. I had almost decided not to stop there after all, in spite of my hope of finding a London publisher. Then, two weeks before my departure, an English lady approached me after the Sunday service at Ananda.

"I shan't be seeing you again, Swamiji," she said. "I'm on my way next week to London."

When she learned that I also was thinking of going there, she promised to meet me at the airport, and, later, made arrangements for me to stay at Centre House. In London she contacted publishers for me, and accompanied me on my various errands about town.

In countless ways, especially on this trip, I've seen God's subtle guidance at work. If therefore these delays in Delhi haven't been a part of my own planning, I think I'd be wise to assume that they may, for all that, have a part in God's plan!

CHAPTER SIX

❋ Swami Narayan ❋

Delhi
December 29, 1972

I'll write now about a visit I made today to a saint, because to-morrow I am going to Ma Anandamayee, and naturally I'll want to write next about nothing but my visit there.

I went today to see one Swami Narayan, in Muzaffarnagar, about seventy miles from here, and a three-and-a-half-hour journey by car. (One can really put on *speed* here in India!) Many people have great faith in him. He is extraordinarily learned — quite probably the most learned man in India, not only in the Hindu scriptures, but in every imaginable branch of knowledge. His library, worth about seven hundred thousand rupees (one hundred thousand dollars), occupies one and a half storeys of a large building, and I'm told he's not only read every book in it, but can refer from memory to exact page numbers. Yet he is extremely simple and modest, so much so that one might easily take him for an ignorant fellow.

Rani and Indu say that whatever he says is infallible; it *must* come true. At least, such has been their experience.

He is also considered one of only four living masters of *Tantra*, a fact which earned him a terrifying reputation in Bengal years ago as a man of vast powers. But I found him very simple, unaffected, and kindly. Certainly he didn't fit the usual conception, my own included, of the Great Saint. And I wasn't there long enough to say that I really formed a *strong* impression. But whatever impression he did make was a good one, and one that got steadily better, to the point where I must say I felt inwardly full of joy by the time we left.

He has peculiar ways, but then I suppose that is a saint's prerogative. Swamiji doesn't want people to feel that he himself has anything to do with the surprising changes that take place in their lives after meeting him. One woman came to him and asked him to help her with a problem: Her son was squandering their family inheritance on prostitutes and drunkenness. Swami Narayan offered sympathy, but no promises. Still, hopefully, the woman urged her son to visit him. And the son did so, more or less as a joke. All he talked about at that meeting was the different girls he had slept with, and the kinds of liquor he liked best. To his surprise, this swami made no remonstrance, offered no pious pearls of advice, and in fact seemed to fall in with the talk like a fellow conspirator.

"You like that girl?" Swami Narayan asked. "You should try this other one. She's *really* good. And have you tried *this* brand of whiskey? The best!" The young man was astounded.

Finally, as he was about to take his leave, Swami Narayan added only one other comment. "How much more enjoyable these things would be," he said, "if it was your own money you were spending on them." It was too mild a statement to make much of an impression. But the swami's real way of working is from within, on the minds of the people he sets out to help. The young man went home full of elation, and told his mother never again to plague him on the subject of his private life, since he was supported in it by no less an authority than Swami Narayan himself.

The following morning he went out and got a job. Since then, and for the past several years, he has been sober, self-controlled, and in every way a model son. He has lost all interest in his former way of life.

I heard several other stories about the swami, similar in nature though not quite so bizarre as this one. One was of a woman who wanted to remarry despite vigorous objections from all her relatives. Swami Narayan spoke to her on their request, but to their dismay he endorsed her marital intentions. She left flashing smiles of triumph in all directions.

The following morning the first thing she said was, "You know, I don't really want to get married again. After all, I have other things to accomplish in life. And I've already had the satisfaction of a happy marriage."

As you may have guessed, Swamiji is not exactly a traditionalist in his religion. Someone he was visiting once argued that it is impossible to remain mentally unaffected by anything that affects the body. Since Swamiji had just claimed the contrary, this man gave him a quart bottle of whiskey and challenged him to drink it all down. Swamiji calmly accepted the challenge, drained the bottle right off, then proceeded to drain another five bottles of the same stuff. One could hardly drink that much *water*, but Swamiji remained quite untouched, and went on conversing lucidly for the rest of the evening.

At learned gatherings, though easily the most learned man present, he always sits unobtrusively at the back of the room, never intruding himself on the conversation except humbly. Yet his authority is widely accepted, and the greatest saints have been known to defer to him.

Though a master of Tantra, he discourages people from following that path. It is, he says, too dangerous for most devotees.

When I first saw him, I had a fleeting thought that this was probably the cook. I found him a chubby man, naked to the waist, gazing with round, uninquisitive eyes through a cloud of cigarette smoke as though not particularly interested in anything going on around him. He greeted our arrival matter-of-factly, then asked someone for a match — as if to say, "So much for introductions." The next thing I knew we were being offered lunch, and he appeared to have lost interest in us.

But it wasn't so; it was only his manner. Soon he came over and joined us. Though he didn't volunteer much conversation he responded kindly enough to my questions. After a few minutes, he asked to see my horoscope — an unusual request from him I am told. He usually refuses to discuss people's horoscopes with them even when they plead with him to do so. ("I'm not an astrologer," is his stock answer, but Rani and Indu both insist he knows far more about astrology than any professional astrologer in the country.)

I then asked him about one of the points on which Swami Muktananda had challenged my Guru. Naturally, there will always be a few differences in techniques between one school and another. Swami Muktananda, however, had made a point of saying that Master's version of a *mantra** was wrong. *Hong-Sau*, he said, is incorrect; it should be repeated the other way around: *So-Ham*. I had suggested a way by which the difference, which seemed trivial enough, might be reconciled. "No," Baba had said, "all the *Upanishads*† say that it should be *So-Ham* not *Hong-Sau*." So, according to him, my Guru was wrong. That did not seem so trivial a matter.

But what could I say, once he backed his claim by reference to scriptural authority? I could feel, and did, that if my Guru had taught the mantra as *Hong-Sau*, his power alone would make it right for anyone who wanted to take it that way, but I couldn't counter this other argument. I don't read Sanskrit.

So now I saw my opportunity. I asked Swami Narayan whether it was true that the *Upanishads* teach *only So-Ham*, never *Hong-Sau*. Swamiji replied:

* A *mantra* is any word sequence believed to have a certain power, usually for self-purification in meditation.

† Key scriptures of Hinduism.

"No, on the contrary, all the *Upanishads* teach it as *Hong-Sau*."

There followed about forty-five minutes of going through various scriptures. One of them, the *Hong-Sau Vidya*, says, "This is the highest mantra." It also calls it "the god of all mantras," and says, "The world is created with it; the world is preserved with it; and the world is destroyed with it."

"By chanting this mantra," the scripture goes on to say, "the seeker quickly attains liberation."

Swamiji went on to say, "Nowhere is *So-Ham* referred to with nearly so much authority."

"Why, then," I inquired, "has it been so much insisted upon?"

"People," he replied, "who don't have an adequate knowledge of the *Vedas* go about creating their own misunderstandings."

But then he added the most vital point of all: "Whatever Guru says is higher than any scripture." (Because it contains his power, and because it is specific for the disciple, rather than something general for all mankind.)

We then talked about my horoscope, which seemed to us really more an excuse for him to open up and speak from his own inner inspiration.

I: "Do you feel I'll be coming back to India someday to build an ashram like the one I've founded in America?"

Swamiji: "You will. Definitely you will. And there will be going back and forth." (The understanding we got was that not I only, but others, would be doing so — in other words, that there would be cooperation between this new ashram and Ananda Cooperative Village.)

I: "When?"

Swamiji: "When your Mars period ends." (This is a reference to a uniquely Indian system which I won't even try to explain here. It is much too complicated.)

I: "Then that should mean in about seven years."

Swamiji: "Sooner. Five years, or even four." He then added, "You will achieve your goal. Even now your path is straight. Don't look to intermediaries. (I assume he meant visiting the saints.) Go straight to God; shake hands with Him."

He corroborated what I myself have felt about this trip, that it is for my own inner development, not really for outward contacts. In that spirit, too, I have wanted to meet the saints. It is in that spirit that I'll be going tomorrow to visit Ma.

(I've received word that Sri Narayan Swamiji left his body in Calcutta on March 28 of this year. How fortunate I was to meet this holy man while he was still on earth!)

Chapter Seven

❋ Ma Anandamayee ❋

Kanpur
January 7, 1973

I've spent the last week here in Kanpur with Ma Anandamayee. It has been a wonderful visit, but I'm afraid you may find my account of it disappointing. Most of the benefit I've received has been internal. Though little has actually happened outwardly, this has been for me in some ways the best time I've ever spent with her.

On previous visits her inner joy overflowed into outward expressions of merriment, delightful wit, almost an eagerness to answer questions and to offer encouragement and helpful advice. Those occasions are among the sweetest memories of my life.

But this time I found her very different — withdrawn, frail, silent most of the time, and speaking only in whispers when she did speak. She was in a car accident several years ago, and has not been in good health since then. Of course, too, she is nearly eighty now. One might say that a lifetime of giving of herself almost twenty-four hours a day would be explanation enough for her poor health, but the truth is that great saints also offer up their own bodies as a sacrifice for others, taking on themselves the karma of their disciples. Ma throughout her life has been a true mother to anyone who ever sought her help. The people whose karmic burdens she has carried must number in the tens of thousands.

I have a feeling that she is nearing the end of this life. At least, I notice in her that same kind of mental withdrawal which I observed in Master during the last two or three years of his life. Ma hardly seems to notice people individually. Her gaze seems abstracted, as though intent on realities hidden from ordinary vision. I think her inner withdrawal is due not only to age and poor health, but also to her own "*kheyal*," or inner impulse.

Kanpur is unfortunately the least suitable of all places to be with her. Crowds of people, completely undisciplined, mill around her every time she makes an appearance. (That alone would be enough to make anyone feel like withdrawing!) She hasn't an ashram of her own here, but is the guest of J.K. Temple (what a name!), and cannot offer guests like me the hospitality that she would give us elsewhere. Kanpur itself, moreover, is a huge, sprawling, dirty industrial city with nothing to recommend it that I can think of. Ma comes here every year for the sake of her local devotees. I've come here for the sake of seeing Ma. The place itself is a no-man's land.

I got off the train last Sunday afternoon, and took a cycle-rickshaw through crowded, dusty streets several miles to the temple. There I found Ma sitting under a huge canopy before thousands of devotees. One Swami Akhandananda, a famous scholar-saint of northern India, was lecturing on the *Bhagavad Gita*. Ma seldom speaks at these gatherings, but still it is mainly her presence that draws the crowds. They consider it a blessing merely to be able to see her. And I know just how they feel. Seeing her there, even from the outskirts of the crowd, I felt immediately uplifted.

J.K. Temple, despite its unprepossessing name, is really a beautiful structure — probably the only beautiful building in Kanpur, though I realize it's unfair to say so since I've seen but a small part of the city. The temple is surrounded by spacious grounds, including a well-kept garden. On one side there are guest quarters. Where we are staying is across the road in a separate compound.

After that first *satsang* I was conducted over to this compound, and there met many old and dear friends.

"Kriyananda! What a surprise! How we have all missed you! It has been what—ten, eleven years?"

A room was hastily cleared for me, with apologies for the mattress on the floor (a huge gymnasium exercise pad, really), the lack of furniture, etc. My goodness, to get even this much at such short notice, and in this place, was real hospitality. I had been uncertain of my plans, and of where to write, so hadn't notified them that I was coming.

Never mind. Soon we were filling one another in on news of the missing years. I chatted with Panu-da, the retired secretary of the organization that has been built in Ma's name. (Ma herself admits to no organizational affiliations.) "We've kept up on you through various visitors," he told me. "My goodness, what a great shock that was to all of us when we heard of your separation from SRF! But I must say, the work that you have been doing since then has been admirable. We've learned of it through many visitors from America."

I showed him and others photographs of Ananda. Everyone seems deeply interested.

Later that first evening I saw one of my oldest and dearest friends in India, Swami Virajananda, a disciple of Ma's since just about the time I was born. We spent an hour or two talking. He used to be very active in ashram affairs, but is somewhat retired now, and is devoting much of his time to solitude and meditation. In fact, most of the old-time disciples seem to have adopted for themselves Ma's mood of inner withdrawal.

For that matter, I, too, have felt withdrawn, especially here with Ma. I got to speak with her first a week ago. I was sitting in the hallway near her room. Word had been taken in to her that I had come. After a little time she came out and greeted me lovingly. But somehow the real exchange was interior, only incidentally external also. It has been that way this entire week. I have stood on the periphery of the throngs, bowing to her in spirit, experiencing so much joy of inner contact that I've felt no need to join the crowds that press in around her, hoping for a smile or a word from her (while she mostly just gazes past them as though they weren't there). Her one body can do only so much. Her spirit can help millions. It is that spirit that I have sought to touch. This in fact has been the essence of my visit here. In it I have found more than blessings enough.

At first I didn't want a private interview with Ma. I was thinking, "She's giving too much of her strength as it is." But finally, when someone asked me if I wouldn't like him to request a "private" for me, I consented. And then, when Ma came out into the hall to talk with me, I found I simply couldn't speak. My heart filled with bliss, and I found myself crying. Ma finally told me again, in a whisper, how happy she was to see me after so many years, and added these words of advice:

"Always try to do your Guru's bidding. Don't accept suggestions from anyone that are in conflict with his bidding."

Other Indian guests, including visiting local townsmen, keep commiserating with me about the narrowness of certain ashram customs. For instance, we Westerners are not allowed into Ma's room here because her drinking water is kept there, and it is believed that our mere presence would pollute it. And of course we must eat separately from the Indian disciples. The other day, a woman disciple was pouring into people's hands, as a blessing, some water that Ma had touched. I wouldn't go out of my way for this kind of blessing, but as I happened to be there I held out my hand for a few drops. The disciple looked at me with consternation, then passed me over. Once more I tried, again without success. Later, on the pleading of other Indians, she sought me out and tried to excuse herself, claiming that she hadn't seen me. But of course she had. What she would not admit for fear of hurting my feelings was that, in her estimation, pouring the water out for me, even without letting the pitcher touch my hand, would have polluted the entire contents of the jug. Water can't be served to Ma if there is a Westerner present. And one evening at the home of some wealthy disciple of Ma's, garlands were carefully presented to all the visiting swamis—all of them, that is, but me. (Afterwards, some man came up to me and introduced himself proudly as belonging to "the very highest of all brahmin castes. Even other brahmins must defer to us." "That's a good start," I replied, "but on the spiritual path one learns that to be a *true* brahmin means inwardly to have found God." I was naive enough to think he'd appreciate my answer, but I'm afraid he was too bound by caste pride to understand my point, supported though it is by the scriptures.)

Many of Ma's devotees have always adhered rigidly to certain Bengali folk taboos, in which I'm afraid foreigners don't figure very well. This narrowness seems in fact to have increased since I was here last. It is mainly a group of Bengali widows who are to blame, and that is pardonable, considering that some of the worst folk traditions of Bengal involve the social exclusion of widows. But when solicitous Indians have come to me and spoken indignantly about these practices, I've assured them that I'm really not offended at all. For one thing, it is good for the ego to be treated occasionally like a pariah. For another, I haven't come here with any desire to be treated particularly one way or another, but only to receive Ma's blessings. As she herself says, "Is it not also a form of narrowness not to be able to tolerate narrowness in others?" If others are ignorant, it seems foolish to increase that all-too-common human commodity by adding to it ignorance of our own.

In fact, a sense of humor should be a part of everyone's mental luggage when traveling abroad. One thing I find sometimes a little difficult to take here in India (and then amusement comes along and saves the day for me) is the tendency of people constantly to interrupt one—and always with the purpose of giving one a lesson. I suspect this is why so many Indians carry on the most casual conversations at the top of their lungs: Only by shouting do they envision any hope of finishing what they have to say! But while everyone talks, few people listen.

The other evening I remarked to someone: "Just look at the temple. How beautiful it is in the sunset!"

Gravely, he turned and informed me, "That's a temple."

I can't begin to tell you how many people, knowing perfectly well that I've been in this spiritual line half my life, have taken pains to explain to me: "You see, we people believe—excuse me, but at least this is *our* sentiment—we believe in what you might possibly call, or at least recognize, by the name of transmigration of souls, or reincarnation."

And the other day, also here in Kanpur, a group of us guests were talking about that ancient book of prophecy that I've described in others of my writings, the *Bhrigu Samhita*, or *Book of Bhrigu*. Written thousands of years ago, this book contains often amazing prophecies about the lives of individuals who hadn't yet been born at the time of its writing. Many of them are living today.*

I started to tell a story in connection with this book.

---

* In 1959 I found myself described in such a way in this book that it would be impossible to apply the same page to anyone else. It even gave, in Sanskrit characters, my Christian name, where I was born, where I grew up, my Guru's name, my monastic name, and events that hadn't yet occurred, but that have since then done so.

"There was a person who once went to the Bhrigu pandit in Benares . . ."

"No," said a Mr. Basu. "That pandit has died."

I: "When did he die?"

Mr. Basu: "About eight years back."

I: "Well, the event I'm describing took place long before that. Anyway, in his reading this man was told that in five years he would lose his life. . . ."

Mr. Basu: "Yes! YES! That is what happens. You see, the *Bhrigu Samhita* tells what is going to come in future. It also tells your past and present. Sometimes . . ."

I: "Excuse me, please. Do you think you might wait until I finish my story?"

Mr. Basu: (conciliatingly) "All right. All right."

I: "Well, this person was told in his reading that in five years he would lose his life. He lived in dread of the time. But at the end of five years he was still very much alive. He quite lost faith in the *Bhrigu Samhita*. Several years later, however, he was traveling in Punjab, and happened to visit the town of Hoshiarpur. There he discovered another portion of the *Bhrigu Samhita* . . ."

Mr. Basu: "Yes! YES! You see, there is another portion of the *Bhrigu Samhita* in Hoshiarpur, in Punjab. There the pandit can't read so well; you have to find your own page. Once I went there with . . ."

Mr. Basu went into a long description of his own experience with the Hoshiarpur portion, perhaps to convince me that this portion really exists. *Quant à moi*, I gave up. Better just to laugh off these constant miscarriages of conversation. Once one does so, they appear quite hilarious.

But while I've got the reader more or less a captive audience (at least you can't talk back to me!) I'll finish the story I was trying to tell.

In Hoshiarpur that man found another reading for himself. In this one it described his former experience with the Benares reading. It then proceeded to give the following explanation:

"At the time when that reading was copied from an earlier version, an important line was left off one of the letters, changing the meaning of the word. Now it read that he would lose his life. But in fact the original had said that he would lose his *property*."

"And is that what actually happened?" the Hoshiarpur pandit inquired.

"It's true," marveled the visitor. "It did. After five years I lost everything I had!"

I had a talk also with Swami Akhandananda, who had been giving daily discourses on the Gita. He is considered one of the foremost Sanskrit scholars in India. I took this opportunity to ask him, too, about the relative merits of the two mantras, *Hong-Sau* and *So-Ham*. He replied:

"The *shastras* (scriptures) instruct one to say *Hong* with the incoming breath, and *Sau* with the outgoing breath. But both mantras are all right, since by repetition *Hong-Sau* becomes *So-Ham*. It is like the story of Valmiki* who, by repeating '*Mara*' (Satan), since he was so evil he couldn't pronounce '*Rama*,' ended up nevertheless repeating the sacred name, '*Rama*.'

"*Hansa* (*Hong-Sau*) is also a scriptural name for the Supreme Lord. It is a *bij* mantra, or seed mantra, and is to be found in the most ancient *Rig Veda*.

"But above all, what Guru says must be done. What Guru says is greater even than the *shastras*.

"There was once a disciple who received a wrong (*ashudha*, or impure) mantra from his guru. After he had recited it for some time, an angel appeared to him and said, 'Your mantra is not right. You

* An ancient sage, author of the great epic, the *Ramayana*.

should say it in this manner.' The disciple very cleverly replied: 'It was by repeating it the way my Guru taught it to me that I got your vision!' After that, what could the angel say?

"The scriptures tell us that even if God Himself is pleased, but Guru is not pleased, that is not enough! Pleasing the guru, implicit faith in the guru—that is everything."

I've spent hours every morning here meditating. It has been a wonderful time for me. Tomorrow I'll be going back with Ma to New Delhi. But I won't stay there. And nor, for that matter, will she. On the tenth I'll be flying to Calcutta.

CHAPTER EIGHT

❋ Calcutta Revisited ❋

Calcutta
January 15, 1973

My visit to Calcutta might be called a sentimental journey. I've had no special purpose in coming here other than the fact that this is where I spent much of my time when I was in India before. It is perhaps the dirtiest, noisiest, most squalid, and certainly one of the most crowded cities in a land of dirty, noisy, squalid, and crowded cities. I always warn visitors to India either to skip Calcutta altogether, or at least not to begin their tour of India here. Why then have I come? And what sort of sentiments do I attach to the place?

But I haven't even told the whole of it. In all of India, Bengal is where I have been treated the most like an outsider. Whereas the people elsewhere have always been eager to hear Master's message through this unworthy instrument, the people of Bengal have always preferred simply to accept the fact of the instrument's unworthiness. (What else? He's not a Bengali!)

During my first year in India I was supposed to devote much time to lecturing on behalf of our society. In Bengal I met with almost no success.

One day I approached one of our directors, who happened to be on the faculty at Calcutta University, and asked him if he could arrange a lecture for me. In reply I got a lecture myself on the high qualifications I ought to have before presuming to address the sophisticated citizens of Bengal.

At last some member of another society, not our own, arranged an intimate gathering for me in a private home, and because somebody's mother or uncle liked what the nice young man had had to say, another talk was arranged for me in a hall in the slum area of Shyam Bazaar. I acquitted myself adequately, and was invited to speak once more, at the Theosophical Lodge. And that, as nearly as I can recall, was the extent of my public activities in this state.

I must admit to a certain sense of personal hurt. Coming to the land of my Guru, and particularly to his own state, I embraced both as if they were my own. I often told people, "My Gurudeva was a Bengali. Guru is the spiritual father; therefore *I* am a Bengali!" But while everyone smilingly approved this sentiment, something — perhaps pride mixed with the inferiority complex of a long-subject people — generally lingered to exclude me. It was not so elsewhere in India.

Perhaps there was a question also of traditionalism. Like most Americans, I don't take easily to doing things merely because they have always been done. But Bengalis especially are steeped in traditions so ancient that no one even considers questioning them. In this kind of setting, I'm afraid I was often at a disadvantage.

And yet, the plain truth is I love Bengal. I love Bengalis. I love this huge, dirty, noisy city. For all their faults (and who doesn't have his fair share of those?) I find a sweetness in these people, a devotional quality that absolutely inspires me. Perhaps it is something in the air. I've been walking down the streets of Calcutta, getting jostled by the throngs, yet drinking in a joy that seems to well up out of the ground. Unbelievingly, I find myself thinking that if any city on earth can be called my city, this incredible place must surely be it!

I arrived here on the evening of the 10th. I had written to an old friend of mine that I was coming, and though I'd had no time for a reply I rather expected he'd be at the airport to receive me. He wasn't. Later I found that a group had in fact gone there to meet me, but had arrived two hours late. There had been some mix-up, either in my instructions or in their understanding.

I've always tried to follow Master's advice: "What comes of itself, let it come." Acceptance without judgment is one of the surest ways to a peaceful heart. So, standing there in the airport terminal waiting for my bag to come through with the other passengers' luggage, I thought, "No matter; Master always arranges something. If my friends haven't come, let's see if it isn't because he has something better in mind for me."

Hardly a moment later someone came up to me and asked, "Where are you from?"

"From California."

"And what is your good name?"

When I told him, he said, "From your face I thought you must be the same person. I have been longing to meet you. A few weeks ago a mutual friend of ours, Mr. Chakrapani Misra, showed me your photograph."

"Mr. Misra! I myself have been wanting to contact him, but I didn't have his address."

"He is staying in Calcutta just at present. I have only just arrived here myself to meet him. I can take you straight to where he is putting up."

Wonderful are God's ways!

Mr. Misra is a friend of mine who was studying for some years at the University of California at Davis. He returned recently to India, and I had hoped to see him on this trip, but was beginning to doubt that I'd get the opportunity. Here was my chance—heaven sent! I stayed in the guesthouse where he was putting up. As it turned out, I would have had a very difficult time of it finding any hotel accommodations at all. Every tourist in India seems to have descended on Calcutta last week.

The next day I was invited to stay in the home of an old brother disciple of mine, Debi Mukerjee, who lived in Master's ashram in Los Angeles the first two or three years that I was there. He is married now, and has three children — a fine family, and all of them deeply devoted to God.

My other friends and I finally got together, too. It was a special joy to see Master's brother, Sananda-da, again.

And much of my time I have spent visiting places where I used often to have to go on work errands during my first year in India. Not much of a sentimental journey after all, you might say! But actually it has been.

One of the charms of India is that human relations mean more here than business does. I made many friends in the shops and other such places when I was here before. The fact that I was a customer was, in their minds, incidental. They would always serve me tea as we chatted on spiritual matters. This time they greeted me like an old and dear friend. One of them, retired a few years ago, insisted that I be brought to his place for tea. None of these meetings will mean much to anyone but me, so I won't dwell on them except to say that they reinforced my appreciation of some of the very real virtues in the Indian character.

Before returning to India this time, I heard much about how the country has changed for the worse. And since coming, innumerable people — Indians — have spoken with disgust of the growing corruption and greed here. No doubt all that has been said has touched on actualities. But other actualities have remained unchanged. There is also great kindness in the Indian character, and sensitivity, and patience, and a quality of natural wisdom — not self-conscious at all. Indians are not at all ashamed, as people are elsewhere in the world, to talk of God and of man's need for Him.

Even in the taxis one sees devotional pictures displayed matter-of-factly. I mentioned to one Sikh taxi driver in Delhi that the people in our *satsangs* love Guru Nanak's song, "*He Hari Sundara* (O God Beautiful!)"

"Of course," he replied, quite simply. "What kind of life is that, when people can't find inspiration singing to God?"

A couple of Indian friends of mine, after returning from a visit to America, expressed their disgust with the radio programs there. "In India," they told me, "you can turn on the radio in the morning and get a program of *bhajans* (devotional songs), followed by a dissertation on the *Bhagavad Gita,* then a talk on spiritual matters. In America all we heard was people singing, 'I love you, you love me.'"

Dr. S. Radhakrishnan, when I visited him in 1961, told me, "A nation is known by the men and women it looks upon as great." An excellent definition. It places a country, not in a static framework of present conditions, but more dynamically in the context of the efforts it is presently making, and therefore of where it is headed. Rome was rich and powerful during the period of its decadence, but wealth and power were its inheritance from the past; decadence was its present reality. It was how people saw things — their corrupted ideals, their ego-centered definitions of greatness, or their cynicism regarding the very existence of greatness — that determined where Rome was actually headed. In the light of Dr. Radhakrishnan's definition, India is a great country.

It is easy for critics to ask, "What is the good of talking spirituality so long as one still cheats one's customers?" Obviously, actions should be brought into harmony with one's ideals. Obviously, also, any nation will be a composite of many human elements. But in my observation the general respect for spiritual values here is deeply sincere, and not merely lip service. Therefore I feel that India has the vitality not only to climb out of her present moral and economic straits, but eventually to surge to the very forefront of international leadership.

It might, I think, be helpful to consider a perfectly average human situation: a young man fortunate enough to be working as a waiter in a restaurant. His salary: a mere rupees sixty—less than ten dollars—a month. On that salary he can't afford to rent a room, so must sleep on the sidewalk. To be poor, indeed, is not always a hardship. Country folk may have even less than this man. But at least in the villages a poor man can maintain a modicum of personal dignity. Poverty in the cities, on the contrary, brings daily reminders of the meanness of one's condition. If that young man should ever reach a point where he earns enough to rent a corner of a small room, he will fear the possibility of a loss of income and a return to the sidewalks with a kind of horror that the average, comfortable American can only dimly imagine. To the Indian, alas, this possibility is only too grimly real.

And then he may want to get married and raise a family. Even more likely, he already has a family. What kind of family life can he build in a tiny room, quite possibly shared with one or two other families? He knows that better things are available to others. And in the movies he sees his heroes living in positive luxury. Fear of destitution and ruin on the one hand, and desire for a minimally decent living standard on the other, drive him almost to desperation.

In the multiplication of millions of such real-life stories lies the sordidness of India's present corruption. If many of the rich are corrupt also, it is because the flower cannot be healthy if the roots are diseased. It is regrettable, but I am too much a friend of these people to call it inexcusable. The fact that they themselves are saddened over it, ashamed of it, is to my mind reassurance enough that they will climb out of it in time. There was a time not so long ago in India when a man would rather lose all his property than tell a lie. India has been thrown off balance by the pressures of modern, competitive society, but once she regains her poise I do not doubt that on a national scale she will *live*, and not merely remember wistfully, the truths that are her greatest heritage.

Before coming here, as I said, I was warned by many that India has changed for the worse, that I would be disappointed. But I am thankful to say that those warnings have not proved justified. India *has* changed, yes. But perhaps so also have I. Perhaps it is only that I am more capable now of appreciating her true greatness, so often hidden as it is. Leaving quite aside the great saints India has produced in every age, including this one, I don't believe any country on earth has produced so many really great men and women in this Twentieth Century—great in an ordinary, worldly sense—as India has. Despite the usual human comedy—I think this is in some cases, if anything, exaggerated here—I find that my love and respect for these people is greater than ever.

And the explanation is simple. No other country on earth in our time has been inspired by so high a vision. Whether this individual or that one measures up to that vision or not, the vision is at least there; its validity is, by the majority, never doubted.

What kind of vision, by contrast, guides our Western nations? Materialism hasn't been the worst of it. Countless numbers of our most admired thinkers claim that life is quite meaningless! The people whom the man in the street in India most deeply admires are great above all in their character, in the purity of their lives, in their simplicity, humility, fair-mindedness, and wisdom.

No, I say this with the fullest sincerity of which I am capable: This is a *great* people, in many ways surely the greatest on earth.

Friday night I took a train 300 miles south to Puri. There I paid my respects to the shrine of my Guru's Guru, Swami Sri Yukteswar. I returned to Calcutta the following night.

Yesterday (Sunday) I was hoping to go out to Dakshineswar to the Kali temple where the great saint, Sri Ramakrishna, lived during the last century. I had no way of getting out there, but this too was worked out for me by Someone who seems to have done a great deal of the planning for this trip. (Very suspicious!)

I was walking down Chowringhee Street. Suddenly a voice hailed me in French. Not imagining that anyone would address me in that language unless he knew that I can speak it, I turned back and replied. I assumed this person must have known me from somewhere. (I didn't recognize him, but then anyone in the public eye is bound to meet innumerable people who know him, on whom he himself draws a complete blank.) Later he confessed he had had no idea who I was.

"But," he said, "you seemed to carry such an aura of peace that I felt I must talk to you." His French was explained by the simple fact that he was French Canadian, and couldn't speak English!

He and his little group wanted to see something of Indian spiritual life during their one-day visit to Calcutta. They asked my advice. And so it happened that I accompanied them as a guide to Dakshineswar, and in that way got to go there myself.

An interesting episode occurred at Kali temple. It was, I'm afraid, my fault. Being Sunday, and also a special festival day, such crowds of people were there that I didn't see the special spots where people are expected to leave their shoes. As a matter of fact, a number of people on the temple grounds *were* wearing shoes, so I, forgetting the custom from my previous visits, assumed that shoes were only to be removed before entering the special shrines. We of course removed them before entering Ramakrishna's room. In another area, however — not a shrine at all — someone began shouting at us that we were defiling sacred ground. Temple guards were summoned. A crowd gathered.

"You — go!" shouted a guard in halting English.

In Bengali I replied, "Look, Brother, we have come here out of devotion, not malice. We removed our shoes before entering Ramakrishna's room, but I didn't realize we should have removed them to enter the grounds themselves. But where there is love, is it right to show anger? Please accept our sincere apologies, and be at peace."

Later, outside, people approached me with indignant cries: "How wrong it was of the officials not to appreciate your devotion!" I thanked them for their consideration, then continued our tour of the area. Fifteen minutes later we returned to find a crowd assembled. Voices were shouting:

"What is more important—love? or mere customs?"

"Yes! What a crime for devotees to be treated so badly!"

"We Hindus have become too narrow in our religion!"

"Yes! Yes! Divine love knows no sectarian boundaries!"

We went later to a house where a well-known Bengali saint, Mohanananda Brahmachari, was visiting. I had met him before, and had in fact been hoping to see him on this visit. It wasn't easy to do so, as hundreds of people crowded near to him for his blessing, but someone grabbed me and wouldn't let me go, somehow pushing and shouting until a narrow passageway was opened up. As I stumbled through, Mohananandaji, looking calm and Christlike, managed to remark through the noise how happy he was to see me again. I was touched that he remembered me at all; our last meeting had been under somewhat similar circumstances. And I was impressed by his obvious poise in the midst of total bedlam.

Yogoda Math, where I stayed for some months on my previous visits to India, happened to be just next door to where Mohananandaji was visiting. I would have liked to visit the old grounds, but Debi Mukerjee had persuaded me that people might misinterpret my motives in going there.

I feel it is perhaps time for me to return to New Delhi.

CHAPTER NINE

❋ Signs and Portents ❋

Delhi
January 20, 1973

I've been here a few days, clearing up some last-minute things.

Indu and I finally went through other channels to find out what has been done about my visa. And at last I can report success. The Home Minister, or his representatives (anyway, someone up there), has said that the Government has realized that the charges against me were absurd, and has ordered that my name be cleared.

Mission accomplished!

Last night we attended a small gathering in someone's home. It was raining gently as we arrived. Everyone said, "This shower is a good omen. Gentle rain when one arrives at any place is like a blessing from heaven."

By the time we left, the rain had ceased. Jestingly, I asked, "Has the blessing been withdrawn?"

"No, Swamiji," Rani replied, "the *shastras* say that if it rains when you depart a place, that is a bad omen." I was astonished.

"You mean this sort of thing is *scriptural*?" Suddenly I recalled Master's writing in his book, *Autobiography of a Yogi*, on the occasion of his boyhood flight to the Himalayas, that that day had begun with "inauspicious rain."

"Yes, Swamiji, scriptural," Rani replied.

"In that case I'd be interested in hearing more about such omens."

"Oh, Swamiji," Indu scoffed, "they're just superstitions!"

"Well, but even at that they'd be interesting."

And so, for whatever meaning they may have for you (Rani believes in them), here are a few other "signs and portents," supposedly scriptural, as Rani dictated them to me while Indu and Dr. Bhan chuckled and swapped jokes in the background.

On Monday and Saturday, don't go east.

Tuesday and Wednesday, don't go north.

Thursday, don't go south.

Friday and Sunday, don't go west.

If you depart a place on Wednesday, you won't return there. This is supposed to be true especially for girls, but Swami Muktananda claims that anyone departing his ashram on Wednesday will never return to it. I was about to leave it on a Wednesday, and he stopped me.

If there is a light shower when arriving at a place, it is a good omen. But if it is raining when one leaves, it is inauspicious.

To see a dead body is a good omen.*

If in your dreams you see a departed person, and he requests something from you, it is inauspicious (a sign of impending death in the family). But if he gives you something, it is auspicious (a sign of gain).

If you dream of a bridegroom's procession (a Hindu custom) it is inauspicious: a sign of impending illness or death. To dream of snakes is also a sign of death.

If you dream of an elephant, it is a sign of coming wealth.

If an owl or a vulture sits on a house (repeatedly, not once or twice merely), it bodes death in the household.

* See page 72.

If crows caw outside your house early in the morning, it signifies that someone special is coming that day.

A comet forebodes famine, or the death of a great person.

An involuntary twitch in the eye, arm, or leg also is supposed to herald news: auspicious, if the twitch occurs on a man's right side or on a woman's left side; inauspicious, if the reverse.

If anyone sneezes just as you are on the point of leaving the house, stop awhile. To leave just then would be inauspicious.

If anyone is going out for some important task, it would be inauspicious for him to call to him from behind, even with the simple question, "Where are you going?"

If one's second toe is longer than the big toe, it is a sign that he possesses a strong will.

If one's ears are large, it signifies that he is fortunate.

And if, when dropping your shoes on the floor, one shoe happens to fall over the other, it is a sign that travel lies ahead for you.

Master had a few such "superstitions," too — brought over, I suppose, from "the old country." Here are several that I happen to remember:

Don't begin a long journey on Thursday afternoon. (This, he once told us, was "according to the word of God.")

Don't leave brooms out where they can be seen. (He claimed they send out "bad vibrations.")

Don't greet anyone the first thing in the morning with one eye closed. If inadvertently you should happen to do so, at once close the other eye also; otherwise some misunderstanding may flare up between you that day.

Gifts should be given and received with the right hand only. (The usual explanation for this common Indian practice is that in India it is customary to reserve the left hand for matters of personal hygiene. I got the impression, however, that Master felt there was a deeper meaning behind the custom. For yogis consider the right side of the body to express a more positive energy than the left. To exchange gifts with the right hand would therefore seem a greater affirmation of good will.)

I recall Master telling a prospective newcomer to his ashram on Mt. Washington that the most auspicious time to arrive would be on Tuesday before eleven in the morning. Whether this was a general principle which others might apply in similar circumstances he didn't say, and I wouldn't hazard a guess on the subject.

And there you have them. Make of them what you will!

I got another kind of "portent" of things to come a few evenings ago. I was invited to join in a panel discussion with a visiting representative from the Vatican. The visitor, a Monsignor Rossano, is in charge of a current Vatican project: the promotion of dialogue with other religions. I was impressed with his personal sincerity. During our discussion, however, I asked him a pointed question.

"Supposing," I said, "in your discussion with the representatives of other religions, you discover that their teachings turn out to have more in common with yours than you have been taught to believe. Would you hail such a discovery as a valuable outgrowth of these discussions? And if you did so, are you confident that you would remain in good standing with the Vatican? Is it really conceivable that your superiors might endorse any conclusion of these dialogues which even mildly qualified the Church's claim to spiritual superiority?

"Would you," I continued, "be willing to meet representatives of other religions with the *prior intention* of discovering what teachings, if any, your religion and theirs hold in common? Or would you from the outset emphasize those points on which you differ? Because if the latter, I see no hope of an honest dialogue, eager though I am to see this sort of thing take place. Anything short of a search for basic similarities would only result in the same old rivalry that has divided religions over the centuries. But I'm afraid that any real effort to explore these similarities would only get you into trouble with your own superiors! It surely is not possible that they have sent you here in quest of evidence that might refute their claim to be the one, true Church!"

"I have come," he replied, "to seek out a basis for honest dialogue. Naturally, we would expect each to want to preserve his own integrity, but beyond that I would of course be interested in finding any real points that we might hold in common."

I was touched, but skeptical. This kind of freedom of conscience is surely not possible within an institutional framework. And then my skepticism was confirmed by several local Catholic representatives.

"Of course," remarked one of them, "the basis of any serious discussion of this sort would have to be a recognition of, indeed even a certain emphasis on, those points on which we are bound to differ."

I decided to excuse myself from any further "dialogues" with the Church on this subject.

I was reminded of what Swami Bharati Krishna Tirth, the late Shankaracharya of Gowardhan Math in Puri, once said to another Catholic monsignor in a supposed debate that someone had set up between them. The monsignor had spoken at considerable length on various Roman Catholic teachings. When the Shankaracharya's turn came to speak, all he said was: "I agree with everything you have said. But I do have one question to ask you: You call yourselves Catholic. Why then do you qualify your name by making it *Roman* Catholic?"

The monsignor had no ready answer. For, obviously, if a thing really is catholic (that is to say, universal), it is a contradiction in terms to restrict its significance by attaching a geographical label to it—or, by implication, to limit it with a narrow set of dogmas.

CHAPTER TEN

❋ Departure from Northern India ❋

Bombay
January 26, 1973

As you see, I have left northern India. It is Indian Republic Day. Lots of parades, radios playing martial music, and widespread (if somewhat low-keyed) excitement. Today I shall be flying south to Bangalore, where I hope to see the well-known saint, Sri Sathya Sai Baba.

My last days in northern India were spent mostly with old friends. What a joy it has been to see them again! The truth is, I had hoped to make them forget me, and hadn't written to most of them in all these years. But now I had to face their reproaches. I tried to make them understand my predicament. My silence, I said, had been from a wish not to draw them into my personal hardships. I had hoped they would go on being loyal to the work to which I had introduced them. But with what tears they answered me! They assured me they had been remembering me every day for all these years, and praying for my eventual return. One man traveled sixty-six hours by train just to see me again. "Nothing," they kept repeating, "has been the same in New Delhi since you left here. Why did it have to happen? Why couldn't this good thing that you were doing have been allowed to continue?"

Everywhere I have gone in India I have heard the same thing, though only in northern India have people spoken of it from such an intensity of personal hurt. I tried to tell them it was all God's will, and also my own personal karma. But what a pain it was for me to discover that so many people have been hurt, and so deeply, on my account. If ever I felt tempted to anger over the seeming injustices of cosmic law, it was that last week in Delhi.

I held one *satsang* in Delhi on Sunday morning, the 21st, and another one that afternoon in New Delhi. The next morning, very early, I took a bus to Patiala, where other old friends had invited me. We held *satsangs* all that day, interspersed with private interviews. I got to bed after midnight, then was up again at 3:00 A.M. the next morning to take the bus back to Delhi. That same afternoon I flew to Bombay.

Altogether, those last few days were a sort of grand finale for my return visit. From here on it will be new ground that I'll be covering.

Here in Bombay I learned that Sri Daya Mata (president of SRF/YSS) was giving lectures at Bharatiya Vidya Bhavan Hall. I had told her I would try to see her in India. This was my opportunity.

Finding the hall filled with devotees, I sat down at the back and meditated while we waited for Daya Ma to come out. At last she did so, and spoke beautifully about the stages on the spiritual path. It was the first meeting of our organization that I had attended in over ten years. I was touched to see so many devotees there. And seeing Daya Ma and two of her sister disciples, all them longtime members of the Board on which I too had served, I could only feel inspired. I thought, "What matter our differences? Those aren't their reality. Their reality is that they love God and Guru, and want to serve them to the best of their ability." In this world of relativity nothing is ever perfect. Only God can bring the bittersweet drama of earth-life to a happy ending—an ending of endlessness in Him alone!

But by faith in Him, also, even life's bitterest experiences become sweet, and we understand that their deeper purpose is only to teach us love—divine love.

Daya Mata, seeing me in the audience, sent word later inviting me to come see her the next day. I did so, and we had a brief but loving reunion, chatting informally, mostly about our recent activities in India. That evening I attended a second *satsang*, as uplifting as the first.

That was yesterday. Today I am flying southward.

As a matter of fact, I had some doubts as to whether I could afford to go to Bangalore. Then a ticket agent at the Pan American office in New Delhi worked it out that I could fly from Bombay to Bangalore and back again at no extra charge. In Calcutta another Pan Am agent insisted that their man in New Delhi had made a mistake, that I should have been charged the full fare for this side trip. But since the ticket had already been written up, he let it stand.

Maybe Sathya Sai Baba just wanted to make sure I made this journey!

CHAPTER ELEVEN

❋ Sathya Sai Baba ❋

Bangalore
January 30, 1973

I came down here on the 26th. I am the guest of Sri N. Keshava, a former member of Parliament and the first mayor of Bangalore, who took Kriya initiation from me in 1961 in Delhi. It has been so nice seeing him again.

But my visit here has turned out to be only an incident in a program of daily visits to Whitefield, a suburb of Bangalore, where Sri Sathya Sai Baba has been staying.

I wasn't actually expecting to have much contact with Baba. Everywhere I've gone in India people have told me that vast throngs always surround him, and that it is almost hopeless to attract his personal attention. Crowds of a hundred thousand are quite usual. People told me of waiting weeks to talk with him, then giving up and going home, or perhaps exchanging only a couple of hurried sentences with him.

But I have been more fortunate. To begin with, the crowds these days have numbered only one or two thousand, not a hundred thousand or more.

And secondly, though I couldn't have done it myself, and in fact tried to stop him, Sri Keshava (that old political leader!) stepped boldly up to some official and asked him to "tell Baba that Swami Kriyananda from America has come to see him."

I was meditating, partly to rise above my embarrassment at having special favors asked for me. Suddenly I felt as though Baba's mind were touching mine. After some time he came out. He saw me right away, and came over with a childlike smile.

"Just a minute, please. I am coming. All right?"

He went around among the other devotees, blessing them, then returned and invited me to come into his house for more private discussions. With that he disappeared into his private grounds. A number of people went with him. When I tried to follow them, a couple of "guards" tried to stop me, but Baba called out, "It's all right. He can come in." Sri Keshava, using me as his cover, came in also.

Sathya Sai Baba is known throughout India. Some people consider him God incarnate. Others consider him a fraud. Just about everyone I've met has had strong opinions either for him or against him. He isn't the sort of person that one accepts casually.

Most of the opinions relate to his miracles, which are nothing if not spectacular. One man I met at Whitefield, a physicist, was converted when Baba poured a little sand into his hands, only to have it turn into a printed copy of the *Bhagavad Gita*. This isn't the sort of thing one turns away from with a stifled yawn. One may believe in it, or one may doubt it; one may say that this isn't what religion is all about; but one will hardly respond to stories like this by saying something like, "Oh well, easy come, easy go."

Baba's most common feat is to produce out of thin air all sorts of objects: candy, ash for medicinal purposes, necklaces, rings. He does it all the time; there's no way he could hold that many objects up his sleeve, or select from among them just what he wants—especially the little spoonfuls of ash that appear, unpackaged, in his palm.

As a matter of fact, such powers are not unique among yogis. Nor, for that matter, are they necessarily a sign of high spiritual attainments. Materializations rarely serve any real spiritual purpose. But before we consider their place in Baba's life and mission, it would be well to ask first how they might be possible in the first place.

The entire physical universe is, as physicists have discovered, a sort of ocean of energy. Material objects are only vibrations of this energy. Differences of vibration cause some vortices of energy to assume the form of a bar of steel, others to appear to our human senses as a loaf of bread. Physicists claim that it should, theoretically, be possible to dissolve a bar of steel into its essential energy, then re-manifest it as a loaf of bread. If they cannot yet perform such feats, it is only because science is not yet sophisticated enough for the task.

One of the stumbling blocks of modern science is its vision of reality as an endless series of separate, static events. It hopes by mastery of all the stages in a particular operation to be able to achieve total mastery of the operation itself. But science is finding that every such stage can be further divided into substages, then *sub*-substages. In every field nowadays the greatest obstacle to integral vision is the growing emphasis on specialization, as each segment of a whole is found to contain a virtually infinite number of subsegments of its own, each one apparently demanding mastery before the whole can be mastered.

I have dealt with this problem at some length in my book, *Crises in Modern Thought*. There I have said that what science has yet to discover is the truth, known to yogis, that it is movement which produces the stages of progress, and not the reverse. To put it more plainly still, it is movement that creates matter, and not the appearance of matter that makes movement possible.

On the face of it, this may sound absurd. How can movement exist unless there is first something to be moved? The answer is simply that primordial movement was a vibration of consciousness. The infinite Spirit is pure consciousness.* That infinite "ocean" of Spirit manifested itself as creation by "moving" a portion of its consciousness, producing separate thoughts and ideas.† As these thoughts moved more vigorously, they produced energy. As this energy became moved more vigorously still, it took on the appearance of matter. But always it is movement that is the essential reality; form is only the manifestation of that movement.

Movements of energy assume various forms by means of the principle of magnetism, which is a natural consequence of any energy-flow. (It is magnetism, for example, that causes whirling vortices of energy to hold together in the form of a leaf. Otherwise the atoms of the leaf would simply dissipate into the atmosphere, and the leaf would disappear.)

In *Crises in Modern Thought* I have pointed out that a bar of iron becomes magnetized—in such a way that we can use its inherent magnetism—when all of its molecules become turned in a single north-south direction.

The billions of molecules in a bar of iron are reoriented north and south, not by some elaborate mechanism which acts upon each of them separately and individually, but simply by subjecting the bar as a whole to the flowing field of magnetism in an already-magnetized iron bar. Advanced yogis, similarly, need only generate a magnetic flow of energy to cause that energy to manifest itself in various material patterns. They need not think, "I must balance this element with that, put this molecule over here and that one over there." Having mastery over the essential elements of magnetic movement (which in turn are only manifestations of still more essential ideas),

---

* Absolute existence in a state of eternal, conscious Bliss, the *shastras* call it: *Satchidanandam.*
† "The spirit of God moved upon the face of the waters." (Genesis 1:2)

they are able to make the outward details of an operation fall into line without actually devoting very much attention to them.

In a similar manner, a competent composer evokes pathos or laughter more by keeping his mind in those states of consciousness while composing than by thinking, "This is the sequence of chords I'll need to create the proper effect: a minor chord here, an anguished dissonance resolving itself there." Always, in every field of endeavor, the most skillful people are those who work with what might be called the "mood" of what they are doing, making the details of their work serve that mood, rather than trying to perfect countless details in the hope of ultimately producing the mood. The more one has of the inner spirit of an undertaking, the more the details simply take care of themselves — a truth which the worldly mind, bowed down as it is by the petty details of daily living, finds it all but impossible to grasp.

Baba only waves his hand, and before one's eyes physical objects appear. If anyone wants to read accounts of these miracles, they are available in the stores in several well-known books about him.

Yet in fact, manifestations of this sort are not necessarily the result of yogic materialization. Once one gets into such abstruse subjects as energy and magnetism, a whole universe of possibilities opens up. Yogis tell us that it is possible by various means to transport already-existing material objects from afar. Rani and Indu told me of a yogi they know in Delhi who can produce medicines out of the air, but they said the medicine bottles all have labels printed in Tokyo, or New York. There are ways of transporting these objects. The most usual method (if something so uncommon can be called usual!) is through the agency of some disincarnate entity.

For the saints of all religions tell us that there exists an astral, or energy universe in which beings like ourselves live much as we do here. Human beings too go there between physical incarnations. It is a real universe, having many levels of manifestation from the lowest hells to the highest heavens. Yogis who call on the services of beings from this universe rarely get the help of highly advanced souls. Some in fact control "elementals," as lower astral beings are sometimes called. To keep the control of such entities requires anything but a high level of consciousness. Though certain powers of concentration are necessary, not every yogi who pulls objects out of the air is a saint.

Most true saints, moreover, are not a bit interested in pulling objects out of the air. They devote their lives to awakening divine love in people's hearts. This indeed is a much more meaningful sort of "materialization"! Usually, in fact, they belittle all public manifestation of miraculous powers as a distraction from the spiritual path, the whole purpose of which is to find God.

Yet to say that anyone who performs such miracles can't be a saint would be to overlook the fact that many great masters *have* performed public miracles. Consider Jesus' feats of turning water to wine at a wedding, and of multiplying a few loaves and fishes into thousands at a large public gathering. God works through His messengers in many, and often unexpected, ways. The real test of perfection is the motive behind one's actions, not the actions themselves. If a saint performs miracles with no thought of personal motive — not even with the thought, "I want to help so-and-so" — but only because the divine impulse in him has chosen to act in that way, he is above reproach.

On the subject of Sathya Sai Baba, India seems fairly evenly divided. Some say his miracles are a purely divine work. Others claim they are ego-motivated. In the latter group, explanations range from suggestions that Baba is a great yogi whose desire for name and fame are obstructing his further spiritual progress, to claims that he controls, and is in turn controlled by, some low elemental. Many also, of course, accuse him of outright fraud.

I myself am not in India on a spiritual "fact-finding mission." It is not vitally important to me whether Baba is genuine or not, or whether he is a great yogi or a fallen one. Moreover, I'm not at all sure that I'm actually qualified to judge him. Not wanting to be involved in this controversy, in fact, I very nearly decided not to come to Bangalore at all. But Sri Keshava would have been hurt had I stayed away; he has been expecting me since November. And many people, both here and in America, have begged me to give them my impressions of Baba.

I have, besides, had still another reason for coming here. Baba, who, I am told, never has any time for writing personal letters, wrote me an inspiring letter a year ago in his own hand. Even though so many people assured me he wouldn't have time to talk with me, I wanted at least a *chance* to express my appreciation to him. And I figured that if he truly is a saint, outward conversation would be unimportant compared to inner, soul-communion.

The worst charge that I heard against Baba, before coming here, was that he materializes objects with the help of a low elemental. This could only mean that he is himself on a low level of development. But in answer to this charge I thought, He does many other things besides materialize things. There are countless reports of miracles of spiritual help and healing that could come only from a high level of Self-realization. He has changed hundreds, perhaps thousands, of lives for the better. He has saved innumerable people from tragedy, oftentimes when they only prayed mentally to him from a distance of hundreds of miles. Miracles such as these are simply not possible for someone who works with a low elemental.

Moreover, Baba's teachings are all of divine love, service, humility, surrender to God's will.

"But anyone can *say* such things!" was the stock answer. "Our scriptures are full of them."

My first impression of Baba, when I saw him, was of a person extraordinarily childlike, loving, full of joy, quite fearless, and completely indifferent to the opinions of others. A tiny man, little over five feet tall, he exuded strength and indomitable courage. Hardly the sort of person, I thought, to indulge in low psychic practices! Everything about him expressed openness, mental freedom, and not the kind of mental bondage that would follow inevitably from consorting with base spiritual associates.

There was a group of about nineteen students from a college in Simla, in the Himalayas. Baba has a special interest in education of the young. He sees in it the key to India's upliftment. (He is also engaged in building a number of model colleges, but more of that later.) Baba called this group into his interview room, and asked me also to join them. Sri Keshava came with me. (Though a native of Bangalore, this was the first time he had ever got a chance to meet Baba!)

Baba spoke partly in Hindi, which I know slightly, and partly in English, which he knows slightly. I could make out most of what he said. It was fresh, original, and wise—certainly not the mere series of frayed scriptural quotations which his detractors had promised me. Only a keen intelligence and an *interested* mind can take old truths and put them in a new way.

"Pleasure is only an interval between two pains," Baba said, referring to the timeless principle of *dwaita* (duality) on which the manifested universe rests. "Pain also is only an interval between two pleasures. Be always non-attached to all opposites if you want to be truly free."

"Happiness lies not in doing what one likes, but in liking what one has to do."

A student tried to touch Baba's feet. Baba discouraged him. "That's just a waste of time," he said with an attractive smile that implied a mixture of scolding and affection. "Devotion must be inward. It must not be an outward show." (So much, I thought, for the claim that all he wants is adulation.)

Baba turned to the teacher who had brought the group. "What time do you get up in the morning?"

"About seven, seven thirty."

Baba wrinkled his nose. "That is too late! Get up at four, four thirty. Have more time for God." (So much, I thought, for claims that he is not interested in people's spiritual development.)

Baba went on to describe the nature of worldly fulfillment.

"One late afternoon a young couple, just married, were walking on the beach by the ocean. Suddenly the groom spied a large thorn just where his beloved was about to place her foot.

"'Look out!' he cried, clutching her to him with an excess of protective concern.

"Six months later they were again walking on the beach. This time, too, he saw a thorn where she was about to step. Pointing at the danger, he said:

"'There's a thorn.'

"Another six months passed. Again they were out walking on the beach, and for the third time he saw she was about to step on a thorn. Annoyed, he cried out:

"'Watch where you're going! Don't you see that thorn?'"

Baba materialized some candy for us. He did it so matter-of-factly, no one looked astonished. It was as if he had taken the sweets out of a bowl. Later, a woman who was also present complained of some physical ailment. A necklace suddenly appeared in Baba's hand.

"Here," he said, sympathetically, "wear this. It will help you."

He also materialized a handful of little photographs of himself, and passed one out to each of us.

With each of these materializations, and with every other that I've been a witness to since then, I've observed no evidence of desire on Baba's part to impress others, no glance about him as if to say, "How do you like *that*, eh?" He appears only as if he were passing candy out to children. My impression is that his entire thought is centered on giving to them, not on receiving anything — even thanks — in return. Close disciples of his have told me Baba considers his materializations quite insignificant — almost as if to say, "Look how easily material objects can be brought into manifestation. Why consider it worth your while to run after them?" He stresses renunciation, non-attachment — attitudes, in short, that are incompatible with an excess of joy in material objects, even in freshly materialized material objects! His own object does not appear to be to excite others with their new possessions any more than it does to impress them with his power to produce the possessions. And it isn't only that he doesn't seem to want anything in return; he won't even accept anything.

"Come to me empty-handed," he tells people, "that I may fill you with what I have to give you — divine love."

To give with a pure motive is, of course, one way of emptying the heart of selfishness, but Baba probably feels that too many people approach the saints with worldly gifts in the hope of bribing them for divine favors.

Several disciples have told me that Baba's materializations, by themselves, would not have impressed them. Repeatedly I've heard the statement from them: "It is his love that converted me."

The only time during my brief stay here that I've seen Baba evince any interest in the impression he was making was yesterday afternoon. He had given a teacher of his local college a letter that he'd composed to the students in English. He wanted to know if his English passed muster. For one whose miracles have made him world famous, I thought this interest in how well he expressed himself in English was rather touching.

After talking to the students awhile, he turned to me with a loving smile.

"Kriyananda, are you well? Happy? How long can you stay?"

"Only three days, Baba, I'm afraid. I wanted to come sooner, but had to go to Delhi about my visa. Now my time in India is running out."

"Oh, too bad." Baba frowned sadly. "But then, in these three days come inside and be here the whole time. We'll have time for private talk, too."

"Baba, I bring you love from many fellow devotees in America, and also in Rome."

Baba smiled gently. Then his look changed to one of indignation.

"Very bad!" he said. "Very, very bad! So many people have tried to hurt you. But don't care for them. Just selfishness and jealousy! Don't care for them. You are on the right path. And you are working selflessly! Oh, very, very bad! Even in religious work there is so much selfishness and jealousy. But you are pleasing your guru. He is always in your heart. Just go your own way."

I was deeply touched. I don't suppose any constructive work is ever done without obstacles of various kinds, including a certain amount of opposition and misunderstanding. I have certainly found it so in my life, particularly in building Ananda. But it is nice sometimes to receive reassurances from people whose opinions are based on deeper-than-usual insight. And Baba has repeated his reassurances every time we've met during the days that I've spent with him.

At the end of that first interview I asked Baba if he planned to come to America.

"No. Too many have gone there in recent years to make money!"

"Then perhaps you could go and help to correct the bad impression."

"First one must put one's own house in order," Baba replied, referring to his present work of building colleges for the upliftment of his own country.

Baba told me he would be going out later that day, so he suggested I come again the following day. I did so, and got in on another group interview. Later, I and several others were invited to have lunch with Baba. And later that same day he granted me a private interview. The third day was pretty much the same, including another private interview, except that it ended with a movie of the opening of a new women's college that Baba has founded.

I was most impressed by this movie. The college buildings are really lovely, and so also are the grounds. Baba is trying by means of these model colleges to influence the educational system of the country, through which he hopes to uplift the general consciousness of the people. He feels, and I strongly agree, that the emphasis in education has become too secular. All his teachers are devotees, not teachers only. And as proof of the all-round merit of his ideals, the students in his institutions score much higher averages than those in other colleges in the country.

I should add, too, that I am impressed with the students as people — with their seriousness, with the respect they show Baba, with their good humor and poise.

This is the direction in which most of Baba's energy seems to be going these days. He has little time left for visitors, except to see them briefly *en masse* every day and bless them. Even though I've had more time with him than most, he has spent the main part of each day in conference with teachers, students, architects, and planners of various kinds working out the details of some new institution.

In our private interviews I didn't actually have many questions to ask. One of my first related to an interesting incident that took place in Sacramento, California, in the spring of 1970.

After one of my yoga classes there, one of my students claimed she had seen Baba sitting with the class. I hadn't seen him, but now I asked him if he had actually been present.

"Yes, definitely I was there," he replied. "That was not imagination."

I also asked him if perhaps now is the right time, with so many of my outward works finished, for greater concentration on my inner life, and for more rapid spiritual development. Baba answered:

"Definitely. Now is the time. Now is the time! That is why you have been drawn here to India, and to see Baba. Baba will flood you with blessings. Before this time you couldn't come. Just see—for ten years you tried to return! But the time was not right. Now it *is* right."

He materialized a necklace for me. One moment his hand was held out; the next moment, it held the necklace. "Wear it always," he said. "It will help your body, and also your mind. It can also be used to heal others." (I'm informed that he has told only two others that the necklaces he has given them can be used to heal others.)

I asked him to bless the members of my community. Baba replied with a sweet smile:

"Of course. That is my duty. I *must* bless them!" He gave me a large envelope full of sacred ash to give to everyone there.

During these three days Baba has shown much love and attention to me—more so, probably, than to anyone else. But what has impressed me most has been the *inner* consciousness that I've felt from him. And when he put this necklace on me, I at once felt blessings permeating me. I realized that the necklace itself was nothing; it was given me only as a vehicle for more subtle blessings.

My meeting with Baba has been an inspiration. I am more than glad I came.

Chapter Twelve

❋ Last Impressions ❋

Rome
February 2, 1973

And so — the long-awaited journey is now all but over. Soon — incredibly soon — I'll be back in the woods and peace of Ananda.

Anticipation usually exceeds fulfillment. But in the case of this journey the opposite has been true. The experience has been even better than I had dreamed.

The chief reason it has been so is that it has given me more than a fond memory to look back on. In some subtle way it has deepened my perceptions — of life, of myself, of God. More clearly than ever I see now that the only thing in life that really matters is to live always in the consciousness of God. Ego-fulfilling interests seem to me now almost inexpressibly petty.

Last November, when I saw that elderly man die at the airport in Rome, I was struck by the uselessness of human efforts to shut out the Great Void. It has struck me also on this journey that one of the differences between India and the West is that Indian culture represents a constant reaching out to embrace that Great Void, while Western culture reinforces the ego's natural inclination to escape it.

On one of my last evenings in India I happened to have dinner in the luxurious restaurant of the Taj hotel, in Bombay. (I almost felt as though I were conditioning myself to face the Western world again.) As I sat there, I asked myself what it was about this place that was so very un-Indian. The luxury? But India is not without its own kind of luxury. The worldliness? But Indians have their fair share of that, too. No, it was rather an atmosphere of isolation from reality—*plastic* is the modern slang word. It reminded me not of the luxurious places in the West, but of every cheap drive-in-off-the-freeway restaurant in America. It had a sort of primness, like a fastidious lady gathering her skirts about her to protect them from the touch of dirty children.

Western civilization has come to view its relations with nature as a competition. It tries to "tame" nature, to conquer it. Western art, music, and literature constantly sound either the theme of defeat in the struggle and the hopelessness of it all, or its counterpart of vigorous affirmation and conquest.

But a conquering nation, when settling the land it has conquered, usually isolates itself from the "natives"—partly to protect itself from attack, and partly no doubt to preserve its own integrity. In day-to-day life in the West one finds the typical practice of conquerors, or at least of people fantasizing that they are conquerors—that of self-isolation from the "enemy," Nature, with countless devices for deluding oneself that the regrettable universe, with its insects and heat and dark nights—and, yes, its eternal call of love to the soul—doesn't really exist except perhaps in the sense of a framed painting on one's living-room wall.

Am I exaggerating? No doubt. To draw a clear contrast one is more or less forced to do so. But there *is* a contrast.

Consider the mood of Indian music. It at least hints at the difference. Indian music is personal, inward: a call of the soul to the Beyond. This too is the basic mood of India.

Indians instinctively try to harmonize themselves with nature, with reality. To aggressive Westerners, the Indian capacity for acceptance appears as passivity. I think I myself was not ready fully to appreciate this quality in them ten years ago. It is a different dimension of consciousness. I needed to be shown, through painful personal setbacks, that one can't succeed always by conquest, that one must learn rather to adapt oneself to reality, and that such adaptation is by no means a euphemism for compromise and defeat.

"What comes of itself, let it come." I have learned over the years, and on this journey perhaps especially, that to ride the currents of life instead of fighting them is the surest way of reaching the shore. I'm not referring to a spineless kind of acceptance. That isn't the teaching of India, either. It requires great self-discipline and self-control to be able to ride the waves without a tumble. But to be in tune with life's subtler currents takes one farther, and brings greater rewards than one can find by forever fighting them.

Every time on this trip that I've let God work out even minor details for me, I've been thrilled to see how perfectly He has done so. It isn't that I've been irresponsible. I've simply considered it my higher responsibility to think of Him, and constantly, consciously to leave the details in His hands instead of fussing and worrying about them as though I alone were the doer. It is like the miracles of Sathya Sai Baba: Move in harmony with the divine energy, and the details effortlessly take care of themselves because they are the natural products of that harmonious movement.

This is the instinctive "mood" of India. Once attuned to it, one notices it in countless little ways — in the birds, for instance, that fly in and out of the homes as though they belonged there; in the bulls that children drive fearlessly through the streets, oblivious of the fact that, in Western countries, the bull has been found to be a dangerous animal. The Indian inherits a culture that says, "Accept reality as it is, harmonize yourself with it, and the very universe will be your friend, your support." Life, like a musical string without an instrument behind it, is thin and inconsequential when it cuts itself off from broader realities.

But India's culture was designed for the gentler pace of village life, of forest ashrams and peaceful gatherings in the open air, where prime emphasis is placed on human and spiritual values. That culture has been thrown off balance by the fierce competition of modern, Western civilization. India at present is a land bewildered.

I am confident this brief phase in India's long history will pass. It *must* pass, for Western civilization itself is finding, even as I have found in my own life, that by competition with reality one may win temporary skirmishes, but never ultimate victory.

For the long run, I believe, it is India's insights into the Art of Living that will bring whatever salvation the human race is entitled to hope for.

❊ About the Author ❊

"Swami Kriyananda is a man of wisdom and compassion in action, truly one of the leading lights in the spiritual world today."
—Lama Surya Das, Dzogchen Center, author of *Awakening the Buddha Within*

A prolific author, accomplished composer, playwright, and artist, and a world-renowned spiritual teacher, Swami Kriyananda (1926–2013) referred to himself simply as a humble disciple of the great God-realized master, Paramhansa Yogananda. He met his guru at the young age of twenty-two, and served him during the last four years of the Master's life. He dedicated the rest of his life to sharing Yogananda's teachings throughout the world.

Kriyananda was born in Romania of American parents, and educated in Europe, England, and the United States. Philosophically and artistically inclined from youth, he soon came to question life's meaning and society's values. During a period of intense inward reflection, he discovered Yogananda's *Autobiography of a Yogi*, and immediately traveled three thousand miles from New York to California to meet the Master, who accepted him as a monastic disciple. Yogananda appointed him as the head of the monastery, authorized him to teach in his name and to give initiation into Kriya Yoga, and entrusted him with the missions of writing and developing what he called "world brotherhood colonies."

Recognized as the "father of the spiritual communities movement" in the United States, Swami Kriyananda founded Ananda World Brotherhood Community in the Sierra Nevada foothills of Northern California in 1968. It has served as a model for nine communities founded subsequently in the United States, Europe, and India.

Dear Reader,

Ananda is a worldwide work based on the same teachings expressed in this book—those of the great spiritual teacher, Paramhansa Yogananda. If you enjoyed this title, Crystal Clarity Publishers invites you to continue to deepen your spiritual life through the many avenues of Ananda Worldwide—including meditation communities, centers, and groups; online virtual community and webinars; retreat centers offering classes and teacher training in yoga and meditation; and more.

For special offers and discounts for first-time visitors to Ananda, visit: http://www.crystalclarity.com/welcome

Feel free to contact us. We are here to serve you.

Joy to you,

Crystal Clarity Publishers

ANANDA WORLDWIDE

Ananda, a worldwide organization founded by Swami Kriyananda, offers spiritual support and resources based on the teachings of Paramhansa Yogananda. There are Ananda spiritual communities in Nevada City, Sacramento, and Palo Alto, California; Seattle, Washington; Portland and Laurelwood, Oregon; as well as a retreat center and European community in Assisi, Italy, and a community near New Delhi, India. Ananda supports more than 140 meditation groups worldwide.

For more information about Ananda's work, our communities, or meditation groups near you, please call 530.478.7560 or visit www. ananda.org.

THE EXPANDING LIGHT RETREAT

The Expanding Light is the largest retreat center in the world to share exclusively the teachings of Paramhansa Yogananda. Situated in the Ananda Village community, it offers the opportunity to experience spiritual life in a contemporary ashram setting. The varied, year-round schedule of classes and programs on yoga, meditation, and spiritual practice includes Karma Yoga, Personal Retreat, Spiritual Travel, and online learning. The Ananda School of Yoga & Meditation offers certified yoga, yoga therapist, spiritual counselor, and meditation teacher trainings. Large groups are welcome.

The teaching staff are experts in Kriya Yoga meditation and all aspects of Yogananda's teachings. All staff members live at Ananda Village and bring an uplifting approach to their areas of service. The serene natural setting and delicious vegetarian meals help provide an ideal environment for a truly meaningful visit.

For more information, please call 800.346.5350
or visit www.expandinglight.org.

CRYSTAL CLARITY PUBLISHERS

Crystal Clarity Publishers offers many additional resources to assist you in your spiritual journey, including many other books (see the following pages for some of them), a wide variety of inspirational and relaxation music composed by Swami Kriyananda, and yoga and meditation videos. To request a catalog, place an order for the above products, or to find out more information, please contact us at:

Crystal Clarity Publishers / www.crystalclarity.com
14618 Tyler Foote Rd. / Nevada City, CA 95959
TOLL FREE: 800.424.1055 or 530.478.7600 FAX: 530.478.7610

EMAIL: clarity@crystalclarity.com

Visit our website for our online catalog, with secure ordering. .

AUTOBIOGRAPHY OF A YOGI

Paramhansa Yogananda

Autobiography of a Yogi is one of the best-selling Eastern philosophy titles of all time, with millions of copies sold, named one of the best and most influential books of the twentieth century. This highly prized reprinting of the original 1946 edition is the only one available free from textual changes made after Yogananda's death. Yogananda was the first yoga master of India whose mission was to live and teach in the West.

In this updated edition are bonus materials, including a last chapter that Yogananda wrote in 1951, without posthumous changes. This new edition also includes the eulogy that Yogananda wrote for Gandhi, and a new foreword and afterword by Swami Kriyananda, one of Yogananda's close, direct disciples.

Also available in unabridged audiobook (MP3) format, read by Swami Kriyananda.

PARAMHANSA YOGANANDA

A Biography with Personal Reflections and Reminiscences
Swami Kriyananda

Paramhansa Yogananda's classic *Autobiography of a Yogi* is more about the saints Yogananda met than about himself—in spite of Yogananda's astonishing accomplishments.

Now, one of Yogananda's direct disciples relates the untold story of this great spiritual master and world teacher: his teenage miracles, his challenges in coming to America, his national lecture campaigns, his struggles to fulfill his world-changing mission amid incomprehension and painful betrayals, and his ultimate triumphant achievement. Kriyananda's subtle grasp of his guru's inner nature reveals Yogananda's many-sided greatness. Includes many never-before-published anecdotes.

Also available in unabridged audiobook (MP3) format, read by Swami Kriyananda.

THE NEW PATH

My Life with Paramhansa Yogananda
Swami Kriyananda

When Swami Kriyananda discovered *Autobiography of a Yogi* in 1948, he was totally new to Eastern teachings. This is a great advantage to the Western reader, since Kriyananda walks us along the yogic path as he discovers it from the moment of his initiation as a disciple of Yogananda. With winning honesty, humor, and deep insight, he shares his journey on the spiritual path through personal stories and experiences.

Through more than four hundred stories of life with Yogananda, we tune in more deeply to this great master and to the teachings he brought to the West. This book is an ideal complement to *Autobiography of a Yogi*.